Invictus

The Way of the

Apostolate

By

David H. Lukenbill

A Chulu Press Book

Chulu Press First Edition published 2010

ISBN-10: 0-9791670-3-5
ISBN-13: 978-0-9791670-3-4

Published by The Lampstand Foundation

www.lampstandfoundation.org

To Doc from Detroit

From Con Air to the McNeil yard, for the miles walked and the years talked, the roads ran and relished, the struggles overcome, the ultimate family joy, and a life lived fiercely, though often wrongly, but, in the end—lived rightly and well.

____ •••• ____

To Marlene & Erika Always

Contents

9

Prologue

Pius XII once stated: "The Faithful, more precisely the lay faithful, find themselves on the front lines of the Church's life; for them the Church is the animating principle for human society. Therefore, they in particular, ought to have an ever-clearer consciousness *not only of belonging to the Church, but of being the Church,* that is to say, the community of the faithful on earth under the leadership of the Pope, the head of all, and of the Bishops in communion with him. These *are the Church...*"(Pope John Paul II. (1988). *CL* #9.)

This book is for penitential professional criminals whose involvement in the criminal/carceral world is of long duration and commitment.

Professional criminals commit crimes for money and live by the ancient criminal way that precludes betrayal of partners or hurting women and children.

To professional criminals, crime is their profession and way of life.

To those professional criminals who are very good—and lucky—at what they do and never get caught, my work will have little value.

It is for those professional criminals who do get caught and serve time in prison, comprising approximately 70 – 80% of the prison population; and who, at some point, may enter a penitential state.

This book is written for them so that through their penance and redemption they may ultimately enter into the apostolate work of reformation to help turn around the statistic that 70% of people released from prison return to prison.

I was born into the criminal world and grew up under its influence, learning that the world was a battleground in which I was on my own. I would have to fight to survive and would have to do whatever was necessary to prosper, and these lessons were deepened and hammered into my soul through twelve years in the carceral world under three separate sentences—two in federal prison for car theft and one in state prison for assault with a deadly weapon.

Later, much later, I was reborn through the waters of baptism into the communal world of the Catholic Church and learned that not only was the world a battleground, the Church was also; but I was strengthened by the knowledge of the three houses of the Church—the Church Triumphant, the Church Militant and the Church Suffering—and that I was a soldier in the mightiest legion of all, the People of God.

As is true in all of my books, I write for my fellow penitential criminals, but this is the only book written for my fellow criminals who are in prison— though if others should find value in my work, and perhaps a new or deeper journey to Rome, I will be very pleased—and the citing, quotations, and references are meant to introduce you to my primary sources within the Catholic canon for much of the intellectual and Catholic journey I pray my books encourage you to embark upon.

Within the criminal/carceral world are many men whose way of life is built upon a strong code of honor which itself is constructed upon their view of the city of man where the rules of success are determined by the prince of the world and it seems evil triumphs, but they have not had the eternal truths of the Catholic magisterium countering the perceived success of evil in the world revealed to them in a context they can accept—a situation unfortunately also applying to many Catholics who have been improperly catechized.

The code of honor—if redirected towards crime-free living—is somewhat congruent with the most devoutly faithful within the communal world of the Catholic Church. I have no objective way of determining how many criminals fall into this group; but based on my 20 years within the criminal/carceral world I estimate that 10-15%

would; and they very often include the top and middle leadership within that world.

It is from this pool of criminals that we would discover those who could become deep knowledge leaders of criminal transformative organizations reforming other criminals, once they are out of prison, or become prison monks if they should spend their entire earthly life in the carceral world.

Deep knowledge is the knowledge that comes from experience, is shaped through education, and informed by Catholic social teaching.

A deep knowledge leader is a transformed criminal with an advanced degree and Catholic social teaching knowledge, working through a grassroots community or prison apostolate, who can help reverse the long-term failure of the criminal rehabilitative effort, as they possess the elemental experiential knowledge of the criminal world allowing them, and them only, the authentic access to criminals long denied the social work professional.

The eight benchmarks of deep knowledge leadership are:

1) Ten years in the criminal world (includes prison) committing crimes for money
2) Five years in a maximum security federal or state prison and not an informant, pedophile, or rapist
3) Ten years out of prison—unless serving a natural life sentence—off parole, crime free, and helping the community
4) Educated about Catholic social teaching
5) Master's degree
6) Leader of a community or prison criminal transformation apostolate
7) Married
8) Catholic

We are describing a person probably in his mid-forties, with an opportunity to work in the development and management of a criminal reformation apostolate serving 70 clients annually for 25-30 years.

This particular work is for all those professional criminals with whom I served time—and those I do not know but by the life they lived—and from whom I have learned much, men of honor and character, who though criminals through and through, live their lives with fierce conviction and stood by those convictions, even in the deepest and darkest pit that prison can sometimes become.

And it is for those men who, whatever their way of life now, live it animated by love and good will, sharing their life experiences with family and friends, and even if not specifically working within the professional field of criminal transformation, still help others avoid the danger and harm they were fortunate to survive.

And it is especially for those men—within prison and without—who chose to enter the professional field of criminal transformation, and through their training, education, and apostolate vocation, bring others to the way of criminal transformation.

The work of criminal transformation is one of spirit and intellect, requiring great physical courage and the ability to work within the ring of the world's fire stoked to soul-searing heat by the prince of the world.

It is a work that requires love for the criminal and the good that can be drawn from the evil that he has brought into the world and a just and strong heart of love to fight the evil that marks his spirit and moves his action.

The way of the apostolate is marked clearly for us within the scripture of the Catholic Church, enunciated through scripture, through the actions of the Triune God, deeply revealing the narrow gate to heaven and the wide road to hell.

The way is for those who understand, having seen the invisible threads driving the affairs of men, that faith is knowledge of the unseen, and the courage to act upon that faith, until the very end.

This book is for those men in prison serving natural life, those rare men who seek to realize a calling to deep spirituality, monastic spirituality, the powerful and consistent prayer life embroidering the lives of the consecrated serving in the Catholic monastery, itself the forerunner of the Western prison, as Skotnicki (2008) notes:

> My own conclusion is that the prison as we know it in the West originated in the penitential practice of the early church and in primitive monastic communities. With some reservations, I argue that it thus bears a meaning as valid and necessary as penance and monasticism themselves. Perhaps a more restrained way of phrasing it would be that since the contemporary prison is in many ways a Catholic innovation, whatever hope it may have as a locus and vehicle of criminal justice lies within the history we are about to survey. (p. 6)

Natural life in a maximum security prison is the point of the spear and a path to an apostolate of greatest possibilities, greatest danger, greatest overcoming; and the spirituality of the prison cell, enfolding a life of prayer, contemplation, study, and teaching is a path to sainthood.

Out of the night that covers me

Out of the night that covers me,
Black as the Pit from pole to pole,
I thank whatever gods may be
For my unconquerable soul.

(*Invictus*—William   Ernest   Henley—1849-1903)

1. God has taught us that we must be able to call

forth our heart of justice against unrepentant evil
and soften our hearts of mercy when penance is
evident.

The masculine heart of the theology of the Church
embraces the righteous rage that drove the
moneychangers from the temple, drove the
inhabitants from the land Israel would inherit, set
Satan behind him as Peter bent to obstruct his
mission, and drove the heel of the woman down
crushing the head of the serpent.

The feminine heart of the theology of the Church is that mercy which forgives 7 times 70, bends the Samaritan knee to lift the stranger, stretches out Christ's hand to heal the beggar, and his great eternal heart to forgive those who crucified him.

The great heart of the Church is engraved with spiritual shock troops, able to go where no priest had gone before, as Chautard (1946) wrote.

> It is very certain that the primitive Church, as we have already hinted, knew how to organize magnificent and numerous shock troops, in the midst of the faithful, and their virtues both struck the pagans with astonishment and excited those most prejudiced against Christianity by their principles, their traditions, and their social background. Conversions were the result, even in circles to which no priest had access. (p. 163)

The great heart of the king of the *Citadelle* protects the souls of the innocent.

> And the mountebank, who shapes beguiling faces by his sleight of hand. That is why I have such an one haled away to execution,

and quartered. Those who watch him at his pranks lose all sense of their domain. But, mark this well, I act not thus out of deference to my jurists who prove the man was wrong. For he is *not* wrong. But neither is he right; nor will I permit him to set himself up as cleverer or juster that my jurists. Also, he errs in thinking he is right; for he, too, sets up as absolutes those newfangled signs of his, clustered and glittering on high, born of his hands but lacking substance, the hallowing of Time, the sanction of religion. His structure has not yet fulfilled itself; but mine has. That is why I pass sentence on the mountebank, and save my people from corruption. (Saint Exupery, 1950, (p. 24)

2. He rises in the morning, calling down the three great armies of the Church—triumphant, suffering and militant—into his vision as he touches his medal ever around his neck, of our patron saint, Dismas, the first canonized saint of the Church, canonized by Christ on Golgotha, and first among those saints leading the forces who make up the Church Triumphant.

He seals his left hand with the sacramental ring of marriage and parental vows taken for eternity, his right hand with the ring of the academy and the vow of a lifetime of learning, and on his wrist the timekeeper binding himself to the hours of the day within which his apostolate is performed, prayers and devotions are rendered, and communion with Christ consumed.

These are his weapons taken to battle, vows of meaning, protection, and spiritual warfare.

He makes the sign of the cross with holy water and then he prays:

Lord Jesus Christ, through the most pure Heart of Mary, I offer Thee all my prayers, works, joys and sufferings of this day, for all the intentions of Your Sacred Heart, in union with the Holy Sacrifice of the Mass throughout the world, in reparation for my sins, and in particular for the intentions of the Holy Father and please protect those being persecuted for our faith all around the world. Amen.

Holy Michael Archangel, defend us in the day of battle; be our safeguard against the wickedness and snares of the devil—May God rebuke him, we humbly pray: and do thou, Prince of the heavenly host, by the power of God thrust down to hell Satan and all wicked spirits, who wander through the world for the ruin of souls. Amen.

God our Father, in your living providence you sent your Holy Angel, to watch over me, to guard me from all evil in light and darkness, all the days of my life and at the hour of my death. Under his protection, and under the protection also of those guardian angels protecting my family, let us and the whole world shoulder our cross, gather our spiritual weapons, and standing with Christ and his Church, fight against evil so that we may live in peace and joy. Amen.

Hail Mary, full of grace, the Lord is with thee; blessed art thou among women and blessed is the fruit of thy womb, Jesus. Holy Mary, Mother of

God, pray for us sinners, now and at the hour of our death. Amen.

Saint Callistus, penitential criminal who became Peter, bless all penitential criminals that they live in the light of God, as did you during your pontifical welcome to the redeemed sinner, and bring peace and guidance in their search for God. Amen

O Jesus, I want you for my sake, because I am nothing, because I am weak, because I am a sinner; for your sake, that I may know you, love you and grow to be like you; for the sake of others, that I may never do them harm, always do them good and give you to them. Since you want me, dear Jesus, take me: all that I have, all that I am and all that I can be. Amen.

With Peter, to Christ, through Mary, for the Greater Glory of God

He goes to daily mass, arriving several minutes early to give him enough time for personal prayers and to read and reflect on the daily readings, prayers and devotions, and to follow the liturgy as it unfolds, reaching its climatic consuming of the body of Christ.

The Eucharist is the height of his reach and the rock upon which he stands; there is nothing more real, there is nothing more powerful, there is nothing more he needs for his apostolate.

Thus spiritually armored and fortified with the divinity of Almighty God, he enters into the daily battle.

3. The field of battle is outside his door and throughout the area within which those he has brought under his care live and attempt to slough off the bonds of sin and live as free men.

It is where he has erected his fortress within which the criminal world no longer rules; within which transformation and conversion is a daily struggle that he always wins, for Almighty God is his beacon, his guardian angel his protector, the deposit of faith his rock, and the magisterium his guide.

4. Each day has its moments and they are broken out into the responsibilities of managing his apostolate by educating the community of his work; sharpening and refining the tools within the apostolate and sustaining it as a learning organization; and building a learning community within which the mission of the apostolate is sharpened, distilled, and communicated to those within and without.

5. To counter our life of criminality and be sustained in our apostolate, and that other penitential criminals may know how our faith is lived—above and beyond our organizational work of preaching the faith and our personal daily practice of communion, scripture, prayer, and rosary—*we must witness our faith endlessly*; cross ourselves when appropriate, wear a crucifix or the medal of our patron saint, hang a rosary from the mirror, share with others our daily practice, speak of the Holy Father and share the words from the great bishops, speak of the social teaching of the Church—*fly the colors*; for they are the bulwark against the demon and the rallying cry for the faint of heart to the banner of our Lord firmly planted in the field of battle, and the strengthening of our eternal soul and that of our apostolate.

6. In all discussions, let the magisterial Catholic perspective, which you have learned and continue to study each day, emerge as yours.

7. We sin at every moment—coveting, denying, carnality—and we counter this with daily practice, with knowledge of our weakness, our need for the Lord and his Church, the rest of our life is penance for our sins which are so deep and so all pervasive that only a lifetime of penance can restore the balance with the people and community we harmed and God who created us; for then we are strengthened and humbled, deflecting misplaced personal honor back to its source, for there is no honor in doing what we must.

8. Our oath of baptism governs our life, is sacred, and cannot be broken, ever:

> We swore to reject sin so as to live in the freedom of Christ's children.
>
> We swore to reject the glamour of evil and refused to be mastered by sin.
>
> We swore to reject Satan, father of sin and prince of darkness.
>
> We swore to reject Satan and all his works and all his empty promises.
>
> We swore that we believe in God, the Father almighty, creator of heaven and earth.
>
> We swore that we believe in Jesus Christ, his only Son, our Lord, who was born of the Virgin Mary, was crucified, died, and was buried, rose from the dead, and is now seated at the right hand of the Father.
>
> We swore we believe in the Holy Spirit, the holy Catholic Church, the communion of saints, the forgiveness of sins, the

resurrection of the body, and the life everlasting.

9. Catholic theologians and philosophers speak of the natural law as implanted upon the hearts and souls of all men, as if Cain and his descendents did not exist, upon whose heart surely the criminal law is what is implanted so much more securely than the "natural."

Rehabilitation efforts continue to fail because the criminal/carceral world blind are attempting to lead the criminal/carceral world sighted, though Christ, in his actions and words—though obscured—clearly pointed to the criminal as the most primary of those to be evangelized with the faith he clarified, and the redemption he brought, to us.

We cannot continue, as a Church, to ignore that the most important sinner our evangelical work must become successful with, is the criminal, for did not Christ confer upon the penitential criminal, Mary of Magdalene, the cloak of apostle to the apostles and the model for penance and did he not canonize as the first saint of the Church, the penitential criminal Dismas.

Who shall we call upon to help us in this work with the criminal if not the reformed criminal, who understands the inner workings of the life within the criminal world and who knows—from having lived it—that the law written upon his heart was the criminal world law, the ancient call of murder, theft, and the lie as the daily word.

10. Criminality is a state of being, as real within the world as sainthood is without and as difficult to transform once set through years of thought and action as its more substantial namesake. Street life, prison life, enriched by endless crimes uncaught for each caught, endless nights running free, fills out the interiority, which only a serendipitous series of events, which may occur, to begin an emptying of the darkness and a refilling with the light.

Our work, your work, is designed to introduce this cognitive disruption by connecting to a continuous relationship of the criminal mind encountering—after years in prison—the sensory and spiritual shock of the outside world in the company of a deep knowledge guide with bones earned inside and outside and a story—the Great Story—to tell that trumps his current criminal narrative.

The Great Story manifests itself from the heart of the Church, as the Second Vatican Council teaches:

> Therefore, the council focuses its attention on the world of men, the whole human family along with the sum of those realities in the midst of which it lives; that world which is the theater of man's history, and the heir of his energies, his tragedies and his triumphs; that world which the Christian sees as created and sustained by its Maker's love, fallen indeed into the bondage of sin, yet emancipated now by Christ, Who was crucified and rose again to break the strangle hold of personified evil, so that the world might be fashioned anew according to God's design and reach its fulfillment. (GES #2)

11. Artists have been writing and making films about the criminal world for generations, revealing its interiority, yet criminal justice and rehabilitative practitioners persist with the assumption that merely with a tweak here, a tweak there—a job, home, school, treatment—all will be right; an idea which ignores the years of revelation of the deep and set culture of the criminal world which no transitory service can change.

12. It is simple to see why the good man accepts obedience to God as normative, but to the bad man, to the criminal, obedience to anyone is abnormal.

The criminal must go his own way and always resist authority, even when locked down at all points, he will resist, often to the death, and it is a way that is sophisticated and hardened, and to assume he can be redirected from a lifetime commitment to a way of life perceived as honorable and true, through jobs, education, counseling, etc., being thrown in his path, is insulting.

13. Identity politics is built upon the ancient principle, like to like, and, though in some cases it is not applicable—as for instance, the ability to analyze the criminal world may be deeper in those outside of it—but in the sense in which we speak of it, the transformation of criminals; that the reformed criminal, and only him, has authentic access to the penitential criminal.

Like to like in this case says that those who *are or have been* can teach what *is or has been,* and what can become.

This seems logical if we understand the truth that all perspectives come from somewhere, and though all are not equally valid, from my dogmatic Catholic perspective; what is valid is that *'being'* is foundational to *complete* teaching, teaching as a pouring out of oneself to one's students or clients.

14. The foundational human anthropology is but two ways: those who wish to serve, follow Christ and those who wish to be served, follow Satan.

15. One result of the wisdom that grows with age is a growing appreciation of the wisdom of the ages and reading Augustine, Aquinas, Newman, and Pius XII, is ageless wisdom indeed.

16. The attraction of evil being something inside of us, as Jung's shadow, or outside of us, as Marx's capitalist, but still responsible for the evil we do rather than our own actions, consciously chosen, is obvious; for how can we be faulted, shunned, negated, if it is not I who am evil, but I who am a victim of evil acting through me.

Catholic teaching resolves this.

Sin has always been defined by the Church as something *done* by an individual:

> Mortal sin requires *full knowledge* and *complete consent*. It presupposes knowledge of the sinful character of the act, of its opposition to God's law. It also implies a consent sufficiently deliberate to be a personal choice. Feigned ignorance and

hardness of heart do not diminish, but rather increase, the voluntary character of a sin. (*CCC2* #1859)

Sin's deepest manifestation—moral evil—has also always been that which is *done* by individuals:

> Angels and men, as intelligent and free creatures, have to journey toward their ultimate destinies by their free choice and preferential love. They can therefore go astray. Indeed, they have sinned. Thus has *moral evil*, incommensurably more harmful than physical evil, entered the world. God is in no way, directly or indirectly, the cause of moral evil. He permits it, however, because he respects the freedom of his creatures and, mysteriously, knows how to derive good from it:

> For almighty God..., because he is supremely good, would never allow any evil whatsoever to exist in his works if he were not so all-powerful and good as to cause good to emerge from evil itself. (*CCC2* #311)

The first sin called forth from God this question to Eve: "Why hast thou *done* this?" (Genesis 3:13) and though Satan was punished—so was man and woman—for angels and humans have free choice and must accept consequences; as in the first crime, God said to Cain "What hast thou *done*? (Genesis 4:10).

Why and *what* and after millennia of human sin, suffering and redemption, we know only too well the *how*.

17. The institutional Church is a human organization and even though founded by God, its human leaders can be corrupted by Satan. For us, the fortress of faith emanating from the institutional Church are when the leaders speak as one, Peter and the bishops, and they have spoken in this way in two universal catechisms, that of St. Pius V, the *Catechism of the Council of Trent* and that of John Paul II, the *Catechism of the Catholic Church*.

Individual priests, bishops, and popes, are to be considered as you consider all clerics, trust but always verify. The history of the human beings in the Church, from the moment of Peter's triple denial, is marked by Satan's influence swirling around the sanctuary of the Church promised by

Christ to withstand for eternity against the gates of hell, against the most evil attempts of Satan to capture it; and it will, but people will stumble, even Peter, and in that respect, treat everyone with the skepticism well-earned in your deep journey through the criminal/carceral world.

Remember always to be guided, in this respect, not by the persons of the Church but the truth of the Church—and this is part of your prayer said each day praying the Rosary—the Apostle's Creed.

> I believe in God, the Father Almighty, Creator of heaven and earth; and in Jesus Christ, His only Son, our Lord; Who was conceived by the Holy Spirit, born of the Virgin Mary, suffered under Pontius Pilate, was crucified, died, and was buried. He descended into hell; the third day He arose again from the dead. He ascended into heaven, and sits at the right hand of God, the Father Almighty; from thence He shall come to judge the living and the dead. I believe in the Holy Spirit, the Holy Catholic Church, the communion of Saints, the forgiveness of sins, the resurrection of the body and life everlasting. Amen.

18. Socialism, the child of communism, and the mark of the truly misled, who see all events as beyond their control, all crimes as caused by others, all good flowing from the omnipresent state, all evil as the result of unbridled individuality; yet the historic continuation of the initial evil—that man is greater than God, that man is God—which Peter, first confronting socialism in 1878, wrote:

> You understand, venerable brethren, that We speak of that sect of men who, under various and almost barbarous names, are called socialists, communists, or nihilists, and who, spread over all the world, and bound together by the closest ties in a wicked confederacy, no longer seek the shelter of secret meetings, but, openly and boldly marching forth in the light of day, strive to bring to a head what they have long been planning - the overthrow of all civil society whatsoever. (*QAM* #1)

> For, while the socialists would destroy the "right" of property, alleging it to be a human invention altogether opposed to the inborn equality of man, and, claiming a community of goods, argue that poverty should not be peaceably endured, and that the property and privileges of the rich may be rightly

invaded, the Church, with much greater wisdom and good sense, recognizes the inequality among men, who are born with different powers of body and mind, inequality in actual possession, also, and holds that the right of property and of ownership, which springs from nature itself, must not be touched and stands inviolate. For she knows that stealing and robbery were forbidden in so special a manner by God, the Author and Defender of right, that He would not allow man even to desire what belonged to another, and that thieves and despoilers, no less than adulterers and idolaters, are shut out from the Kingdom of Heaven. (*QAM*, #9)

In this eternal revolt against the father, emanating from Satan, the socialist of today marks the criminal justice system as a tool of the rich against the poor; and the uninformed criminal eager for a reason other than accepting the responsibility of his own choice governing his criminal life, perhaps in a plea for mercy or public favor among the academics, goes along to get along, violating his own hard fought source of honor in standing strong in his own actions, doing the time for the crime if need be, though always seeking an honorable way out.

19. Marxist ideology is not, in any way, philosophical grounds for reformation from criminal world ethics as its ideology is built on the concept that capitalism is theft—criminal in its being—and its reality has been a reign of tyrants stealing freedom, life, and vitality from the people they rule.

20. We see, in the books by many former criminals, language used that is based on Marxist assumptions alien to the criminal world, the largest alienation being that criminals want to leave the criminal world—an assumption continually negated by the narrative of the books these authors write, pleasing to the socialist, captivated by the stories of violence, lust, and intoxication, lives for which they secretly yearn—a narrative embracing the obvious remaining criminality.

21. The Catholic way is the only way out and it is a daily rhythm of prayer and battle with the deep bonds of the satanic life lived so long, which always clings to us, inviting us to return to the deep sleep.

22. In our daily practice we are upon the ancient path to that wonderful place, that mythical place of legend and dreams, where we pray unceasingly and Pope Benedict XVI (2007) provides instruction.

> The more prayer is the foundation that upholds our entire existence, the more we will become men of peace. The more we can bear pain, the more we will be able to understand others and open ourselves to them. This orientation pervasively shaping our whole consciousness, this silent presence of God at the heart of our thinking, our meditating, and our being, is what we mean by "prayer without ceasing." (p. 130)

23. We are hard-wired towards God, as Fr. Tugwell (2010) notes, and it is not a wiring of control but of following our deepest desires, which are towards the call to sainthood foundational to human nature.

> The ideal is for us not to control our appetites at all, but to allow them full rein in the wake of an uncontrolled appetite for God. It is important to take seriously the implication of our beatitude that there really is an appetite for God, and for his righteousness. We all too easily speak and

think as if righteousness resulted chiefly from the curbing of our appetites, as if our appetites were only for sin. But strictly speaking we have no appetite for sin. What we experience as an appetite for sin is a sick appetite which has mistaken its object. In moments of despondency we may perhaps look around and think that we should be much happier if we gave up trying to be good, if we could enjoy all the vices of the world around us. But that is only a fantasy. The desire to goodness is really a much more robust desire that any alleged desire for evil...We must be content to grow slowly towards goodness, taking, if need be, a long time to convalesce. Most of us, maybe, will still be barely at the beginning of our recovery even when we die. But that is better that killing ourselves pretending to be healthy...

Saint Thomas says desire is the faculty which receives, so that the bigger our desire is, the more we can receive...Our part in this life is to learn to want largely and earnestly enough to make us capable of the infinite rightness of God's kingdom...The more we try to tame and reduce ourselves and our desires and hopes, the more we deceive and distort ourselves. We are made for God and nothing less will really satisfy us.

So we must allow our innate appetite for infinity to dislodge us whenever we are inclined to settle down and call it a day. (pp. 316-317)

In the fell clutch of circumstance

In the fell clutch of circumstance
I have not winced nor cried aloud.
Under the bludgeonings of chance
My head is bloody, but unbowed.

(*Invictus*—William Ernest Henley—1849-1903)

1. The suffering of the criminal is caused by the results of his own acts—he is never innocent—of predation upon the innocent which drive him farther and farther from God; and for the penitential criminal, the suffering he has caused will flow through him like an angry river for a very long time—perhaps forever.

2. The great knights, still suffering in purgatory for their sins, being purified for the triumphant entry into heaven, always knew that the central stone upon which the chivalry of their knightly oath, the protection of women and children, rested, was that they—as armed and trained men—had the over whelming strength to protect the women and

children from evil men, and only they, the knights possessed this power, for women and children rarely possessed such strength.

3. Like bonds to like, deep calls to deep. As children of God we are called to realize what we are, and in our realization, what we are to become.

4. Do not become a traitor, a Judas. Do not walk in partnership with a man and then betray his secrets, for did not our Lord teach:

> The Son of Man indeed goes, as it is written of him, but woe to that man by whom the Son of Man is betrayed. It would be better for that man if he had never been born. (Matthew 26:24)

When you no longer are a criminal, at that point forward, then your cooperation with the policeman is right and just, but betrayal from looking back, other than in the confessional, is not.

5. Read the reports of the stumblings of the men and women—laity and religious, the humble and the mighty—of the Church to remind you of Christ's promise that the gates of hell shall not prevail against her.

The battle is already won, but we, to be among the victorious forever, must continue the lifelong battle within ourselves.

6. In the constant calls from teaching to bow down to God is the truth that because of our original sin, we all physically die and become as the dust.

7. Being criminals, we will spend a very long time in Purgatory, unless we burn in the fire of suffering through the cross, refining our nature in service, and reaching to heaven through our evangelization.

8. Suffering, a unique thing we criminals bring upon ourselves, and deliver to others, often reveling in the transmission, can be reflected upon in the story of Job, which John Paul II does:

> 12. The Book of Job poses in an extremely acute way the question of the "why" of

suffering; it also shows that suffering strikes the innocent, but it does not yet give the solution to the problem.

Already in the Old Testament we note an orientation that begins to go beyond the concept according to which suffering has a meaning only as a punishment for sin, insofar as it emphasizes at the same time the educational value of suffering as a punishment. Thus in the sufferings inflicted by God upon the Chosen People there is included an invitation of his mercy, which corrects in order to lead to conversion: "... these punishments were designed not to destroy but to discipline our people".

Thus the personal dimension of punishment is affirmed. According to this dimension, punishment has a meaning not only because it serves *to* repay the objective evil of the transgression with another evil, but first and foremost because it creates the possibility of rebuilding goodness in the subject who suffers.

This is an extremely important aspect of suffering. It is profoundly rooted in the entire Revelation of the Old and above all the New Covenant. Suffering must serve *for conversion,* that is, *for the rebuilding of goodness* in the subject, who can recognize the divine mercy in this call to repentance. The purpose of penance is to overcome evil, which under different forms lies dormant in man. Its purpose is also to strengthen goodness both in man himself and in his relationships with others and especially with God. (*SD* #12)

9. Though prison will rarely be the world where we walk the true path— except perhaps for those who are doing natural life—it is the world where we can begin the process of learning around the issues connected to our life of crime, punishment, suffering, and will.

Great works abound for study.

The collection of timeless literature that has played a large role in the development of my thinking around criminal reformation is a transformative tool that can be used as a guide for those criminals seeking to restructure their lives.

While some of this literature, prevalent during the period (1940's – 1970's) when the carceral world was beginning to shape the criminal world—though still relevant today and tomorrow—will have perhaps been replaced by newer works, the essential message will have remained the same, if perhaps more graphic.

This brief bibliography is for transformed criminals, who are able, through inclination, redemption, education, and skill, become a grassroots organizational leader who can generate the transformation of other criminals.

It is directed to penitential criminals who are Catholic or potential converts who, because of their leadership in the criminal world, will have significant success and impact in the work of criminal transformation.

It is directed to those individuals who committed crimes for money—professional criminals—to whom crime was a way of life and prison time an occupational hazard.

It is a small box or two of books that will open the doors of perception while in the cells of deception.

Benton, W. (1960) . *Never a Greater Need*. New York: Alfred A. Knopf.

Benton, W. (1968). *This is My Beloved*. New York: Alfred A. Knopf.

De Ropp, R. S. (1968). *The Master Game: Pathways to Higher Consciousness Beyond the Drug Experience*. New York: Dell Publishing.

Exupery, A. d. S. (1950). *The Wisdom of the Sands*. New York: Harcourt, Brace and Company.

Frankl, Viktor E. (1984). *Man's Search for Meaning*. New York: Simon & Schuster.

Frazer, J.G. (1959). *The New Golden Bough*. (Gaster, T. H. Ed.). New York: Criterion Books.

Ginsburg, A. (1956) *Howl & Other Poems*. City Lights Books; San Francisco.

Gurdjieff, G. I. (1973). *Beelzebub's Tales to his Grandson: An Objectively Impartial Criticism of the Life of Man: First, Second & Third Books*. New York: E. P. Dutton.

Hoffer, E. (1966) *The True Believer*. New York: Perennial Library.

Irwin, J. (1970). *The Felon*. New Jersey: Prentice-Hall.

Kennedy, Daniel B. & Kerber, August. (1973). *Resocialization: An American Experiment*. New York: Behavioral Publications.

Kerouac, J. (1999). *On the Road*. New York: Penguin Books.

Khayyam, Omar. (1970). Translated by Edward Fitzgerald (Fourth Version). *The Rubaiyat of Omar Khayyam*.

Le Bon, G. (1952). *The Crowd: A Study of the Popular Mind*. London: Ernest Benn Limited.

Maugham, W. S. (1954), *The Razor's Edge*. Garden City, New Jersey: Garden City, New York.

Nietzsche, F. W. (1954). *The Portable Nietzsche*. (W. Kaufmann, Trans.). New York: Penguin Books.

Sartre, J. P. (1963). *Saint Genet: Actor & Martyr*. New York: Pantheon Books.

Watts, A. (1972). *The Book On the Taboo Against Knowing Who You Are*. New York: Vintage Books.

Watts, A. (1970). *Psychotherapy East & West*. New York: Ballantine Books.

Wilson, C. (1982). *The Outsider*. Los Angeles: Jeremy P. Tarcher, Inc.

10. One of the powerful realities of prison is that you are encouraged to bear what suffering you do, to accept that you have brought it upon yourself, and to respect its voice, doom may seem imminent but that will pass; all that matters is how you stand under the sword of impending doom, unafraid and primed for battle, or cowering in the cold corner of fear drenched marble.

The carceral world is a primer in the bearing of the cross of suffering upon which great Dismas hung, beside the Lord, who brought him to heaven, and made him the first canonized saint of the eternal Church now on earth, the criminal, the thief, the penitent.

And on that day of Golgotha, another penitential criminal, Mary of Magdalene, stood at the foot of the cross of wood, the tree of life, the arc of heaven, the two criminals embracing our Lord at the moment of his ascension.

Beyond this place of wrath and tears

Beyond this place of wrath and tears
Looms but the Horror of the shade,
And yet the menace of the years
Finds, and shall find, me unafraid.

(*Invictus*—William Ernest Henley—1849-1903)

1. Four men have stood on the ground of the world through time and history, and each spoke his truth:

I am a prophet, said Moses,

I am an enlightened man, said Buddha,

I am God, said Christ,

I am a prophet, said Mohammed.

From each sprung a mighty religion, but only one is eternal and true and which door will you go through.

Only Christ named his predecessor, by spiritual root and word, *and today* we are with him each day at the table of the mass in the world which he instituted as the mass of heaven.

> In the earthly liturgy we take part in a foretaste of that heavenly liturgy which is celebrated in the holy city of Jerusalem toward which we journey as pilgrims, where Christ is sitting at the right hand of God, a minister of the holies and of the true tabernacle; we sing a hymn to the Lord's glory with all the warriors of the heavenly army; venerating the memory of the saints, we hope for some part and fellowship with them; we eagerly await the Saviour, Our Lord Jesus Christ, until He, our life, shall appear and we too will appear with Him in glory. (*SC* #8)

Only Christ named his successor:

> 13. Now when Jesus came into the district of Caesarea Philippi, he asked his disciples, "Who do men say that the Son of man is?" 14. And they said, "Some say John the Baptist, others say Elijah, and others Jeremiah or one of the prophets." 15. He said to them, "But who do you say that I am?" 16. Simon Peter replied and said, "You are the Christ, the Son of the living God." 17. And Jesus answered him, "Blessed are you,

Simon Bar-Jona! For flesh and blood has not revealed this to you, but my Father who is in heaven. 18. And I tell you, you are Peter, and on this rock I will build my church, and the gates of Hades shall not prevail against it. 19. I will give you the keys of the kingdom of heaven, and whatsoever you bind on earth, shall be bound in heaven, and whatever you loose on earth shall be in heaven." (Matthew 16:13-19)

Jaki (1997) takes us there, to that moment and that place:

The Old Testament had its series of great heroes and saints, who acted like stability incarnate, but none of them was called rock, let alone given the name Rock...

....Simon was declared to be the Rock itself. The phrasing was so unmistakably Aramaic as to exclude the possibility of later forgery. The scenery of the words, "And on this Rock" is somewhat conjectural, though worth exploring. The huge wall of rock over the source of the Jordan was visible to anyone "in the neighborhood of Caesarea Philippi." On the top of that rock there glittered Jupiter's temple; below, next to the source of the Jordan, there was a cave, a famous sanctuary of Pan. Jupiter and Pan were the great symbols of state worship and nature worship, the two perennial deadly traps for fallible man. Jesus indeed could hardly have chosen in the entire land a better backdrop for His words that the Jaws of Hell shall not prevail over His Church built on Peter, the Rock. (pp. 112-113)

And Peter is with us still, though being a different man called by God when it is time, though often stumbling as men do, yet remaining now for two thousand years, the Rock.

2. The shock troops of the Catholic Empire were many and some of the mightiest came from the soldier Ignatius:

When Loyola sent his protégés out unto "the battleground of faith," he gave them as their watchword..."I am made all things to all men, that I might by all means save some." ...They were the most brilliant courtiers, the sternest ascetics, the most self-sacrificing missionaries and the sharpest traders, the most devoted footmen and the shrewdest statesmen, the wisest confessors and the greatest impresarios, the most gifted physicians and the most skillful assassins. They built churches and factories, sponsored pilgrimages and conspiracies, proved theorems in mathematics and stated propositions in church dogmatics, worked to suppress the freedom of enquiry and made a

host of scientific discoveries. They were—in
the broadest possible sense of the term—
truly capable of anything. (Barthel, 1984, p.
10)

From these martial saints, Loyola foremost among
them, come the tools and sensibilities that govern
our work, shape our days and nights, and guide our
steps within the dark wars of the criminal and
carceral world.

They have given us tools of remembrance and
prayer, devotion and adoration, to hold us to the
single truth, the single service, to Christ and his
Church; with Peter, to Christ, through Mary, for the
greater glory of God.

So much of the focused boldness personified by the
Jesuits over the centuries is what is necessary for
this work which others—for whatever reason—do
not embrace with consistency, scale, and skill.

3. If we judge truth by the currently advancing
power of secular institutions over the Catholic
Church, we align ourselves with the gates of hell—

with whom we shall always strive, but never succumb—as Christ promised.

We must always hold to the high road of Church history—the road of loving and protecting the innocent, retaining hope and guided by our faith in charity—the road occupied by the saints and under the standard of Our Lord Jesus Christ following the three steps to virtue; as noted by St. Ignatius:

> Hence, there will be three steps; the first poverty as opposed to riches; the second, insults or contempt as opposed to the honor of this world; the third, humility as opposed to pride. From these three steps, let them lead men to all other virtues. (SE #146)

We do not trek on the low road, where dissent, fear and chaos rules, guided by the desperate prince of this world whose three steps to evil are noted by St. Ignatius:

> The first step, then, will be riches, the second honor, the third pride. From these three steps the evil one leads to all other vices. (SE #141)

4. The pacifist looks to the selected aspects of the words of Christ in the New Testament for affirmation that God is a God of *only* love, peace, and mercy and he is all that; but he is also the God of the Old Testament, the trinity with Christ and the Holy Spirit a God *also* of rage, war and vengeance; truly a God for all, truly a God able to defeat the enemy in spiritual and temporal combat.

As the great story settled into the souls of Catholics revealing ancient truths, various strategies of Satan attacked, from within and without the Church.

They are the heresies, yet all have the one satanic root; that angels and men know more than their creator.

Murray (1960) writes about pacifism.

> It does not assert that war is intrinsically evil simply because it is a use of force and violence and therefore a contravention of the Christian law of love promulgated in the Sermon on the Mount. This is absolute pacifism, an unqualified embrace of the

principle of non-violence; it is more characteristic of certain Protestant sects. The relative pacifists are content to affirm that war has now become an evil that may no longer be justified, given the fact that no adequate justification can be offered for the ruinous effects of today's weapons of war. Even this position, I shall say, is not to be squared with the public doctrine of the Church. (pp. 249-250)

The "relative pacifists" for whom "war has now become an evil that may no longer be justified" because of the destructive power of nuclear weapons, are those surrender-to-evil souls who also feel capital punishment is no longer justified because of advancements in prison technology—the super-max prison.

5. The way of the pacifist is the way of death. It is the way of all the great heresies, it is the way to the reign of evil in the world, for in the protection of innocent human life, and in respecting the dignity of all human beings, the primary protection is towards the dignity and life of yourself, and as you would give your life for that of your friend, you must fight to the death to protect your own.

The way of the pacifist removes action from the individual—within whom the eternal law, set into the human soul by God, informs the temporal actions human beings take in response to evil—and invests action within the state, whose human-made law bends and shapes itself around the whims and wisps of the politics and degraded morality of the criminal city, the city of man.

Pacifism as national policy is utopian, perfection only attainable from the return of Christ, the divine king holding the sword of ultimate justice in his righteous hand.

Socialists, who always proclaim pacifism yet still see the strike against capital as just war; indeed to them, wars of labor against capital are just wars.

A cousin of pacifism—formed from the same socialistic roots—is the concept of restorative justice, where the essential Catholic truth of punishment for crime is replaced with the idea of restoration, as one of the founders of the restorative justice movement, Howard Zehr (2002) claims.

> The modern field of restorative justice did develop in the 1970s from case experiments in several communities with a proportionately sizable Mennonite population. (p. 11)

> Restorative justice has brought an awareness of the limits and negative by products of punishment. Beyond that, however, it has argued that punishment is not real accountability. (p. 16)

Punishment cannot be replaced for it lies at the center of Catholic anthropology, and without it there is no accountability.

Adam and Eve were punished by being driven from the garden, Satan was punished by being driven from heaven, and Cain was punished by being driven from his home and family.

The *Catechism* teaches:

2266 The efforts of the state to curb the spread of behavior harmful to people's rights and to the basic rules of civil society correspond to the requirement of safeguarding the common good. Legitimate public authority has the right and the duty to inflict punishment proportionate to the gravity of the offense. Punishment has the primary aim of redressing the disorder introduced by the offense. When it is willingly accepted by the guilty party, it assumes the value of expiation. Punishment then, in addition to defending public order and protecting people's safety, has a medicinal purpose: as far as possible, it must contribute to the correction of the guilty party. (*CCC2*)

6. Criminal justice, the discipline, is that of seeing justice rendered to criminals, the justice of their due; the justice of maintaining their dignity as human beings created in the image of God; the legal justice flowing from their criminal acts; and the rcdemptive justice emanating from their penance; all flowing from the spiritual foundation upon which the cardinal virtues—prudence, justice, fortitude, and temperance—stand:

Justice: The cardinal moral virtue which consists in the constant and firm will to give their due to God and to neighbor. (*CCC2*, p. 885)

7. We encounter in the Old Testament a martial perspective—but not, as some would proclaim, due to the higher level of barbarity of that time—but to the eternal need for man to fight evil, as the world remains, now as then, a battleground between good and evil.

Today it is even a more perilous battleground as the satanic truth envelops us in clouds—the greatest victory of the devil is to have convinced us he does not exist. This is why—though so many want only to look to the New Testament for guidance, somehow believing Jesus Christ was absent from the Trinity during the Old—as fighters in the eternal battle, raging always most fervently within the sanctuaries of the Church itself, Catholics must embrace both Testaments in the war against evil, for they are really only one.

102 Through all the words of Sacred Scripture, God speaks only one single Word, his one Utterance in whom he expresses himself completely.

> You recall that one and the same Word of God extends throughout Scripture, that it is one and the same Utterance that resounds in the mouths of all the sacred writers, since he who was in the beginning God with God has no need of separate syllables; for he is not subject to time. (*CCC2* 102)

8. We can not allow ourselves to become distracted; through our knowledge of the powerful connection reformed criminals have with the early roots of the Church, with the fullness of the ministry of Christ, as Guardini (1956) notes about Mary Magdalene.

> Is Jesus siding with the harlot against the Pharisee?—with the life of dishonor against lives of decency and order? Certainly not. But he is exposing the self-satisfied accuser in all his worldliness as one who is cold, hard, blind, and deeply enmeshed in the prejudices of his class. Simultaneously, he reveals the true position of the woman they

so cruelly judge: the depths of her contrition, the heights of her love place her, the redeemed one, on the plane of her Redeemer, far above anyone present. The woman whom you call sinner, Jesus seems to say, ceased to be a sinner before she entered this room; for no one can love as she loves who has not already been forgiven for sins that were great indeed.

Here is no romanticizing of sin, no siding with passion against law and order. The Savior demonstrates sharply that for him one thing only is important: the human being, whether its name is Mary Magdalen or Simon the Pharisee. Both are addressed here, not as they measure up to worldly standards, but as they measure before God. This sinner was one of the very few who really believed. Was there any other besides the Lord's own Mother, Mary of Bethany and John?

Jesus does not champion the cause of the free individual against society. He does not stand for the heart as against the law. He does not side with the outcast against the prudent and the respected. He does not consider the sinner as much more valuable that the virtuous. Jesus is far from both romanticism and class-consciousness. He is interested only in the individual soul whom he places before God. He possesses the godly power that springs from divine freedom, power to stir all manner of men: the poor and lost simply by accepting them as human beings and bringing them the tidings of God's mercy; the great and admired by making them realize that they dangerously overrate themselves and risk losing their salvation." (Guardini, p. 58)

9. The way to triumph lies here, take it, surround yourself with the word, it is not the book but the word, from holy souls, who may not know they are holy, who know that only God can make that judgment, we can only follow the path before us, stumbling, haltingly, as the creatures we are, but always towards the Church triumphant. Guardini (1956) again:

> No one has the right to judge whether or not another lives according to the spirit of the Sermon on the Mount. There is no specific outward behavior that expresses it. Indeed, not even the chosen one himself can be certain how things stand with him. St. Paul says it explicitly: God alone is judge. Dare then to hope that you are chosen! The chance is taken in faith, and neither from the world's point of view, nor from that of inner or outer experience, is there any possible objection. But I cannot love my

enemy? You can bring yourself to the point of no longer hating him. That is already the beginning of love....I can't even do that!...Then try at least to keep your dislike out of your speech. That would be a step in the direction of love....

But surely that would be watering the wine? Isn't it a question of everything or nothing? To be quite frank, the Either-Or people seldom appear to practice their own severity. Their uncompromising attitude often looks suspiciously like rhetoric. No, what the Sermon on the Mount demands is not everything or nothing, but a beginning and a continuing, a rising again and plodding on after every fall. (pp. 94-95, ellipsis in original)

10. Love, as Jesus taught us, is to follow the Great Commandment (Mark 12:28-31) of loving God and our neighbor, but loving our neighbor does not include the criminal, for he has set himself outside the law, becoming an outlaw. To those who are aggressors against the person and property of the innocent, what applies is not the great commandment but the eternal teachings of the Church embodied in justice and mercy. To apply the great commandment to the aggressor is the way of death—the way of the pacifist who is merely raising up victims for the predatory aggressor.

11. For most of the years of the 2,000 years the Church has been on earth, she swam in martiality, with papal temporal leadership of armies but a few centuries behind us and spiritual leadership closer still, and holy war was embraced by Peter, as Tyerman (2006) notes:

> In the later eleventh century, holy war became a particular and intimate concern of the reformed papacy, one which was to transform Christian attitudes and practices for half a millennium. (p. 45)

12. True knighthood has been, is now, and will be for all time, the sole act of defending Christ and those he loves.

13. The theology of the body is the theology of husband and wife, knight and lady of the realm.

14. The Great Commandment to love God and our neighbor is practiced by loving that which is God, within ourselves and others and recognizing that which is of the devil, within ourselves and others, and fighting against that with righteous anger and destroying that; else we are like warm milk against the bitter cold of space, a momentary sop soon overtaken.

15. St. Thomas Aquinas revealed God to us as the prime mover—unmoved—and at each moment of essential decision it is so—pause—stop—death—battle—contemplation—meditation—here is the core of religion, the unmoved.

> Therefore it is necessary to arrive at a first mover, put in motion by no other; and this everyone understands to be God. *ST,* (Q2/A3)

16. The great German Jesuit, Alfred Delp, who was a leader in the anti-Nazi Resistance, was executed in 1945, and his writings from prison are powerfully prophetic, reminding us of the world and the desert:

> Blessed is the era that can honestly claim that it is not a desert wilderness. Woe,

however, to the era in which the voices calling in the wilderness have fallen silent, shouted down by the noise of the day, or prohibited, or drowned in the intoxication with progress, or restricted and quiet out of fear and cowardice. The devastation will soon take over so horrendously on all sides that the scriptural reference to a *desert wilderness* will spontaneously occur to us all. I think we know this. (Delp, p. 24)

Isn't today, in the world, an approaching desert? Surely from the cold concrete and steel of the streets and the prison it surely is, and what do we pull from the desert, what great discipline and courage can it call forth from us.

Many years ago, while serving time in McNeil Island Federal Penitentiary, a group of us formed a study group to read writers whose works resonated with us, and one we chose was Antoine de Saint-Exupery's book *The Wisdom of the Sands*, reflections of a desert king. Here are the opening words.

All too often have I seen pity led astray. But we who govern men have learnt to plumb their hearts, and we bestow compassion only on what is worthy of our concern. No pity waste I on the shrilly voiced afflictions that fret women's hearts. As I withhold it from the dying and from the dead. And I know wherefore.

A time there was, in my young days, when I pitied beggars and their sores. I hired physicians and procured balsams for them. Caravans from a far-off island brought me those rare unguents laced with gold that mend the torn skin above the flesh. Thus did I until the day when I discovered that beggars cling to their stench as to something rare and precious. For I had caught them scratching away their scabs and smearing their bodies with dung, like the husbandman who spreads manure over his garden plot, so as to wean from it the crimson flower. Vying with each other, they flaunted their corruption, and bragged of the alms they wrung from the tender-hearted. (p. 3)

17. God does not know what is to happen, no more than we with our children. He must trust in what he has taught us—and that we learn to call upon him—as we trust in what we have taught our children once they are out in the world.

18. The real is not what we can see, feel, touch, or taste, only envision, imagine, dream, pray for, and ultimately it becomes the rock of granite, the mountain of stone we stand upon within the world as he once stood and stands still, the only one who says I am God, I am he. The others, the heretical prophets, seers, and enlightened men, those seekers after God who stand in their midst, are blinded to him by the ancient pride, that human pride that believes God is not—that only man is— for he we can see, feel, touch, and taste.

19. The responsibility we have in our apostolate was taught us by Pope John Paul II:

> In the context of Church mission, then, *the Lord entrusts a great part of the responsibility to the lay faithful, in communion with all other members of the People of God.* This fact, fully understood by the Fathers of the Second Vatican Council, recurred with renewed clarity and increased vigor in all the works of the Synod: "Indeed, Pastors know how much the lay faithful contribute to the welfare of the entire Church. They also know that they themselves were not established by Christ to

undertake alone the entire saving mission of the Church towards the world, but they understand that it is their exalted office to be shepherds of the lay faithful and also to recognize the latter's services and charisms that all according to their proper roles may cooperate in this common undertaking with one heart" (*CL* #32)

20. The professional criminal is the strong man, unafraid to die for what he wants, with no fear of the darkness and silence; and once transformed through the blood of Christ, and forged through the combat theology of the carceral/criminal world, may join with one who is a stronger man yet, the truly faithful priest, the ascetic, unafraid to die for what he believes, who walks with Peter through Mary to Christ; and together—criminal and priest— they can recover those who are lost, together they can recover an essential aspect of the Christic mission, to the deep sinner, to Saint Mary Magdalene and Saint Dismas.

Adam (1935) teaches us:

The new era, the Kingdom of Heaven, has come. Therefore the least in this Kingdom of Heaven is greater than John (Matthew 11:11). Jesus can testify: I saw Satan like lightning falling from heaven (Luke 10:18). The strong man is bound and the Kingdom of Heaven has free passage (Matthew 12:29)

21. The Church on earth, the Church administered, represented, and continued by sinful human beings, is always being attacked and it is always being corrupted, so if it is to these stumblers you look to for validation of your faith, you shall always be disappointed.

The Kingdom of heaven was inaugurated on earth by Christ. "This kingdom shone out before men in the word, in the works, and in the presence of Christ." The Church is the seed and beginning of this kingdom. Her keys are entrusted to Peter. (*CCC2*, #567)

22. One often hears from Catholics, who are defending their dissenting positions on a myriad of issues traditionally held by the Church, that if we but listened to what Christ was teaching us in the New Testament...all would be well. This is a refuge of the heretic who forgets Christ is a member of the

Trinity, and from the Trinity came the complete covenants embodied in the Old and New. Testament, all of which still stand, as interpreted and taught by the Catholic Church

23. In the end, it is a spiritual war between those who believe in God and his teachings embodied within the Catholic Church and those who do not, those who live by the ways of the world, those who accepted the choice—rejected by Christ—from Satan to embrace the world.

The way of the Catholic is the way to eternal life in heaven. The way of the world is eternal life in hell.

It matters not how strait the gate

It matters not how strait the gate,
How charged with punishments the scroll.
I am the master of my fate:
I am the captain of my soul.

(*Invictus*—William Ernest Henley—1849-1903)

1. **I**n the end it is always back to each of us and the mastery we have over our life, which is only real when we *realize* that to which our life is most founded upon, the divinity and eternalness of God.

2. As the institutions defining and sustaining morality and honor break down, we are thrown back upon ourselves—and new honor groups—to maintain our blood connection to Holy Mother Church, for, as Bowman (2006) notes, the collapse also creates.

> As ideas of morality were in the course of being transferred from the normal proccooco of enculturation to the realm of mere personal preference, the effect on honor of that primacy of the individual conscience

was in a way even more devastating. Conscience, at least, really *is* individual, and those who sought to live by an idiosyncratic standard of personal and individual morality—as who did not?—could always appeal to conscience as a justification. But honor by its very nature subordinates the individual to some larger community and is therefore inseparable from its social and communal dimension. Without an honor group in whose eyes the individual sought to distinguish himself, there could be no honor. After the collapse of the official culture, there remained small and local honor groups—the neighborhood, the office, the profession or trade group—but of general agreement, often even within the groups themselves, as to what kind of behavior was to be regarded as honorable. In some—such as street gangs, prisons, police and some military units—there was a regression to more primitive forms of honor that were in part a reaction to the disappearance of more sophisticated and socially validated ideas of honor. (pp. 242-243)

The ancient honor group of the Church, centered around the Church Militant, the Church Suffering, and the Church Triumphant, bowing to the great table of the mass of the world, partaking of the divine flesh and blood of God, earthly knights eternal in the work only ending with the opening of eternity to all of the faithful with the coming of our Lord.

3. I have always known that the only path to personal transformation from the criminal/carceral world to the communal world, was an interior path, and if transformation was to occur, it must become the only path in life, and so it has been for me and so it must become for those who take on this charge: help your brothers.

> Where does this motivation come from?...I heard the same story again and again. Someone had experienced an intense kind of pain that branded them in some way. They said, 'I *had* to do this. There was nothing else I could do.'
>
> At some moments in their lives, social entrepreneurs get it into their heads that it is up to them to solve a particular problem. Usually something has been brewing inside for a long time, and at a particular moment in time—often triggered by an event—personal preparedness, social need, and historical opportunity converge and the person takes decisive action. The word "decision" comes from the Latin *decidere*, meaning "to cut off." From that point on, the

social entrepreneurs seem to cut off other options for themselves.

Over time, their ideas become more important to them than anything else. Every decision—whom to marry, where to live, what books to read—passes through the prism of their ideas. Although it is probably impossible to fully explain why people become social entrepreneurs, it is certainly possible to identify them. And society stands to benefit by finding these people, encouraging them, and helping them to do what they need to do. (Bornstein, 2004, pp. 240-241)

4. Whether in prison or out, honor and truth is paramount and the ancient way of the Catholic Saint, to Christ through Mary, for the greater glory of God—in the great teaching of the Church that the strong protect the weak, thou shalt not harm the innocent nor betray thy brother, justice prevails eternally though not in this world, yet we are called to be just, prudent, courageous, and temperate, loving God and the way of the Saint.

5. It is never the living persons of the Church we follow, but the communion of saints—for there are only two perfect human beings, Mary and her son Jesus—and even Peter stumbles.

It is Peter the Pontiff, not Peter the man, and it is Christ who Peter follows, not himself, for Peter is captive to the teaching, to Christ, God the Father and the Holy Spirit, and through Mary—Human Mother of God—lies the eternal path.

I see a remainder mark on the book of John Paul II, *Crossing the Threshold of Hope.* And how indicative of the words of Simeon so long ago:

> And Simeon blessed them and said to Mary his mother, "Behold, this child is destined for the fall and rise of many in Israel, and to be a sign that will be contradicted. (Luke 2: 34)

The Catechism teaches:

> Faith is first of all a personal adherence of man to God. At the same time, and inseparably, it is a *free assent to the whole truth that God has revealed.* As personal adherence to God and assent to his truth, Christian faith differs from our faith in any human person. It is right and just to entrust oneself wholly to God and to believe

absolutely what he says. It would be futile and false to place such faith in a creature. (*CCC*2, 150)

It is dogma we can trust, the eternal truths of the Church and they are outlined for us in the two great universal catechisms, of Trent and Vatican II.

From the Catechism of Vatican II:

The dogmas of the faith

88 The Church's Magisterium exercises the authority it holds from Christ to the fullest extent when it defines dogmas, that is, when it proposes, in a form obliging the Christian people to an irrevocable adherence of faith, truths contained in divine Revelation or also when it proposes, in a definitive way, truths having a necessary connection with these.

89 There is an organic connection between our spiritual life and the dogmas. Dogmas are lights along the path of faith; they illuminate it and make it secure. Conversely, if our life is upright, our intellect and heart will be open to welcome the light shed by the dogmas of faith.

90 The mutual connections between dogmas, and their coherence, can be found in the whole of the Revelation of the mystery of Christ. "In Catholic doctrine there exists an order or hierarchy of truths, since they vary in their relation to the foundation of the Christian faith." (*CCC2*, 88-90)

6. Through the revelatory movements of the Great Story we see the eternal cathedral in time, the True Church, founded by God, who came to earth as man that we might know.

The others, the heretical and paltry resemblances of truth which go under names of men and whim are, as Burnett (1860) describes:

> Protestantism is not exclusive. Its leading principle, from which all others logically and necessarily flow, is studiously adapted to flatter individual pride, and indulge the will. Its soft and flexible gum-elastic character admits of infinite modifications without any efficient checks, and easily confirms itself to the prevailing sentiment of each succeeding age. Progress and Reform being its leading ends, it never finds rest, so long as the human mind loves novelty, and seeks excitement in change. (p. 376)

The Catholic Church stands today as it stood over 2,000 years ago, and the Holy Mass today follows the same form as that of the apostles, as does the organization of the temporal church itself, arranged hierarchically under Peter.

7. Abolishing capital punishment is abolishing the fight against evil—surrendering to evil—for if evil is not worth fighting, nothing is.

The Church has become masterful at doing good but struggles fighting evil; and that is to be expected as a Church founded by God yet managed by humans, for whom even the recognition of evil often eludes them let alone the constancy of fighting it.

Evil did rule the ancient world before Christ and hangs on by its bloody talons yet today, but ever since he came, it has been in retreat and it lost its once mighty hold upon the world when the majority of human beings were no longer in real slavery.

8. In many ways my generation was a wasted generation, in its intoxicants, its overwhelming propensity to hate authority, its addiction to sensuality, its fear of Catholic truth and its corruption of institutions, yet from this waste grows good flowers and rich grasses.

9. Today, as we walk into the world, let us be within our armor, as the samurai:

> Every morning the samurai...would bathe, shave their foreheads, put lotion in their hair, cut their fingernails and toenails, rubbing them with pumice and then with wood sorrel, and without fail, pay attention to their personal appearance. It goes without saying that their armor in general was kept free from rust, that it was dusted, shined, and arranged.
>
> Although it seems that taking special care of one's appearance is similar to showiness, it is nothing akin to elegance. Even if you are aware that you may be struck down today and are firmly resolved to an inevitable death, if you are slain with an unseemly appearance, you will show your lack of

previous resolve, will be despised by your enemy, and will appear unclean...

Although you say that this is troublesome and time-consuming, a samurai's work is in such things. It is neither busy-work nor time-consuming. In constantly hardening one's resolution to die in battle, deliberately becoming as one already dead, and working at one's job and dealing with military affairs, there should be no shame. (Tsunetomo, (2002) p. 39)

The Lampstand Foundation

The Lampstand Foundation is a 501(c)(3) nonprofit corporation founded in Sacramento, California by David H. Lukenbill in September of 2003 as a lay apostolate grounded on the social thought of the Catholic Church to provide leadership development tools for community organizations—managed by reformed criminals—working to reform criminals. Lampstand provides education about Catholic social thought, criminal transformation, and grassroots organizational management, to deep knowledge leaders, nonprofit organizations transforming criminals, their community of support, and the public.

Vision

Inspiring criminals who have transformed their lives, secured college degrees, and returned home to Rome; to reenter the community and show others the transformative path, and how the pain of suffering can become the power of teaching.

Mission

Transforming the repentant criminal, suffering from his distance from God, into a deep knowledge leader who can teach other criminals the path to redemption through the Catholic Church.

Core Beliefs

Suffering transformed builds souls. Just as the muscle tissue tearing that leads to greater physical muscle growth resulting from body building, suffering is soul tearing which, through redemption, allows soul growth.

1) Deep knowledge leadership—college-educated, transformed criminals, professionally trained to manage criminal transformative organizations—will dramatically improve the effectiveness of criminal transformation.

2) Catholic social thought forms the intellectual and spiritual foundation of criminal transformation.

3) Grassroots criminal transformation organizations need ongoing access to capacity building services.

4) Business and professional leadership, working to create community social capital through the transformation of criminals, will benefit from gaining knowledge about Catholic social thought.

Goals

We want to facilitate the leadership development of penitential criminals whose personal transformation, education, and reconciliation or conversion to Catholicism has inspired them to seek graduate degrees, professional organizational training, social teaching training, and assume a leadership role in the community helping other criminals transform their lives.

1) To inspire educated and transformed criminals who are baptized Catholics and want to help others, gain a graduate college education and professional training.

2) To provide capacity building tools to criminal transforming organizations about Catholic social teaching, start-up planning, strategic planning, fund development, board development, communications & marketing, and for profit business development.

3) To educate the business and professional community about the leadership capability of educated, transformed criminals and the use of Catholic social teaching as a transformative tool.

Apostolate Principles

1) *We will defend innocent human life in all that we do.*

80 Reason attests that there are objects of the human act which are by their nature "incapable of being ordered" to God, because they radically contradict the good of the person made in his image. These are the acts which, in the Church's moral tradition, have been termed "intrinsically evil" (*intrinsece malum*): they are such *always and per se,* in other words, on account of their very object, and quite apart from the ulterior intentions of the one acting and the circumstances. Consequently, without in the least denying the influence on morality exercised by circumstances and especially by intentions, the Church teaches that "there exist acts which *per se* and in themselves, independently of circumstances, are always seriously wrong by reason of their object". The Second Vatican Council itself, in discussing the respect due to the human person, gives a number of examples of such acts. "Whatever is opposed to life itself, such as any type of murder, genocide, abortion, euthanasia, or wilful self-destruction, whatever violates the integrity of the human person, such as mutilation, torments inflicted on body or mind, attempts to coerce the will itself; whatever insults human dignity, such as subhuman living conditions, arbitrary imprisonment, deportation, slavery, prostitution, the selling of women and children; as well as disgraceful working conditions, where people are treated as mere instruments of gain rather than as free and responsible persons; all these things and others like them are infamies indeed. They poison human society, and they do more harm to those who practise them than to those who suffer from the injury. Moreover, they are a supreme dishonour to the Creator." (Pope John Paul II, 1993, *Veritatis Splendor* #80)

2) *We will work for social justice in all that we do.*

1928 Society ensures social justice when it provides the conditions that allow associations or individuals to obtain what is their due, according to their nature and their vocation. Social justice is linked to the common good and the exercise of authority.

1929 Social justice can be obtained only in respecting the transcendent dignity of man. The person represents the ultimate end of society, which is ordered to him:

What is at stake is the dignity of the human person, whose defense and promotion have been entrusted to us by the Creator, and to whom the men and women at every moment of history are strictly and responsibly in debt.

1930 Respect for the human person entails respect for the rights that flow from his dignity as a creature. These rights are prior to society and must be recognized by it. They are the basis of the moral legitimacy of every authority: by flouting them, or refusing to recognize them in its positive legislation, a society undermines its own moral legitimacy. If it does not respect them, authority can rely only on force or violence to obtain obedience from its subjects. It is the Church's role to remind men of good will of these rights and to distinguish them from unwarranted or false claims." (*CCC2*, #1928-1930)

3) *We know that our work is with, and through, the community.*

In our time, *the role of human work* is becoming increasingly important as the productive factor both of non-material and of material wealth. Moreover, it is becoming clearer how a person's work is naturally interrelated with the work of others. More than ever, *work is work with others* and *work for others*: it is a matter of doing something for someone else. (*CA* #31)

4) *We know that Catholic social thought is a transformative social force.*

2419 "Christian revelation...promotes deeper understanding of the laws of social living." The Church receives from the Gospel the full revelation of the truth about man. When she fulfills her mission of proclaiming the Gospel, she bears witness to man, in the name of Christ, to his dignity and his vocation to the communion of persons. She teaches him the demands of justice and peace in conformity with divine wisdom.

2420 The Church makes a moral judgment about economic and social matters, "when the fundamental rights of the person or the salvation of souls requires it." In the moral order she bears a mission distinct from that of political authorities: The Church is concerned with the temporal aspects of the common good because they are ordered to the sovereign Good, our ultimate end. She strives to inspire right attitudes with respect to earthly goods and in socio-economic relationships.

2421 The social doctrine of the Church developed in the nineteenth century when the Gospel encountered modern industrial society with its new structures for the production of consumer goods, its new concept of society, the state and authority, and its new forms of labor and ownership. The development of the doctrine of the

Church on economic and social matters attests the permanent value of the Church's teaching at the same time as it attests the true meaning of her Tradition, always living and active.

2422 The Church's social teaching comprises a body of doctrine, which is articulated as the Church interprets events in the course of history, with the assistance of the Holy Spirit, in the light of the whole of what has been revealed by Jesus Christ. This teaching can be more easily accepted by men of good will, the more the faithful let themselves be guided by it." (*CCC 2* 2419-2422)

5) *We know that corporal works of mercy are essential to comfort the suffering, and that spiritual works of mercy are essential to stop the suffering.*

2447 The *works of mercy* are charitable actions by which we come to the aid of our neighbor in his spiritual and bodily necessities. Instructing, advising, consoling, comforting are spiritual works of mercy, as are forgiving and bearing wrongs patiently. The corporal works of mercy consist especially in feeding the hungry, sheltering the homeless, clothing the naked, visiting the sick and imprisoned, and burying the dead. Among all these, giving alms to the poor is one of the chief witnesses to fraternal charity: it is also a work of justice pleasing to God:

> He who has two coats, let him share with him who has none and he who has food must do likewise. But give for alms those things which are within; and behold, everything is clean for you. If a brother or sister is ill-clad and in lack of daily food, and one of you says to them, "Go in peace, be warmed and filled," without giving them the things needed for the body, what does it profit? (*CCC 2*, 2447)

Guiding Criminal Justice Principles

1) ***Broken windows policing works***. Allowing even the minor violation of a broken window in an area helps create the impression of an environment where law and order does not prevail and where crime flourishes. Responding quickly and efficiently to all crimes, regardless of the perceived state of seriousness or other local community concerns, is the foundation of good police work.

2) ***The response to crime should be timely, balanced, and just.*** When justice is for sale, either through wealth, influence, or ideology, a fertile soil is created from which crime grows. The training and education of professionals in the criminal justice system is built on a foundation of traditional and well-reasoned concepts of justice and it needs continual reinforcement to remain an effective response to crime.

3) *Prison is an appropriate criminal sanction to protect society and punish the criminal, while allowing the opportunity for criminal reformation.* Prison is an effective sanction for crime which has been used by human beings since ancient times. It serves to protect the public from predatory crime, acts as a deterrence and as incapacitation, and allows the penitential criminal the opportunity—while removed from the community—to reflect upon and correct his criminal behavior.

4) *Capital punishment is an appropriate response to the criminal evil of murder, rape, and pedophilia.* Capital punishment is often the only effective social method available to protect the innocent and applied with dispatch after legal review of the crimes charged and determining the fitness of its application, should be considered an appropriate sentence for murderers, rapists and pedophiles; who, knowing the time of their death, are able, with certainty of their remaining time to do so, seek God's forgiveness. Five states, as of May 2008, already approve the use of capital punishment in child rape cases: Louisiana, Montana, Oklahoma, South Carolina, and Texas.

5) *Repentant criminals deserve a second chance.* Excepting those cases of serious predatory behavior deserving the death penalty or natural life in prison, repentant criminals, once they have clearly shown—over a ten year period after being released from criminal justice supervision—that they have transformed their life by becoming a productive member of their family, their church, their work, and their community, should be allowed to apply for a complete pardon in a simple straightforward process.

6) *It takes a reformed criminal to reform criminals.* For generations the ability of non-criminals—even those with the highest professional and academic credentials—to effectively rehabilitate criminals has proven, based on sound evaluations, to be virtually non-existent. Recruiting reformed criminals who have, through education, training, and the development of a deep knowledge leadership approach to criminal transformation, may well succeed where others have failed. Considering the current recidivism rate of 70%, and with the consensus that peer-based help does, at the very least, attract those who want help to transformative programs, it is time to try this approach in a substantial enough way, over time and properly evaluated, to discover if we can rely on it as a valuable tool for large-scale implementation.

7) *In the work of criminal reformation, it is vital to keep in mind that the criminal—not society, capitalism, or the criminal justice system—is the problem.* Some criminal justice advocates take the position that among the people connected with the carceral world, the good guys are the criminals and the police, district attorneys, prison guards, and the legislators who support stringent criminal sanctions, are the bad guys.

This is the absolutely wrong position, for in virtually any carceral population in America it is the criminals who are the indisputable bad guys, while the good guys are the ones protecting the public from the depredations of criminals. Those who parlay the myths of Hollywood or Marxism into an intellectual stance that fails to understand this basic fact, does everyone a disservice—in particular the penitential criminal—who may find little reason for proper expiation within a culture defining criminality as somehow admirable.

Program

Lampstand's direct teaching work is supplemented by a monthly e-letter, quarterly newsletter, an annual policy primer research report released on the feast day of St. Dismas on March 25th, an annual book from Chulu Press (a Lampstand imprint), and periodic monographs.

Leader's Circle

This is a transformed criminal association whose purpose is to develop and support deep knowledge leaders. Membership is restricted to individuals fulfilling the following eight life benchmarks: 1) Ten years (includes prison) committing crimes for money; 2) Five years in a maximum security federal or state prison; 3) Ten years out of prison, off parole, crime free, and helping the community; 4) Educated about Catholic social teaching; 5) Master's degree; 6) Leader of a community criminal transformation program; 7) Married; and 8) Catholic.

David H. Lukenbill, President
The Lampstand Foundation
Post Office Box 254794
Sacramento, CA 95865-4794
Phone (916) 486 – 3856
E. Dlukenbill@msn.com
W. www.lampstandfoundation.org
B. www.catholiceye.blogspot.com

Rosary for the Criminal

Table of Contents

Introduction

One of the most powerful spiritual weapons of the Church is praying the Rosary.

In *The Catechism of the Council of Trent*, first published in 1566 by Pope St. Pius V—who established the feast of the Holy Rosary on the anniversary of the naval victory won by the Christian fleet at Lepanto, October 7, 1571, which was attributed to the help of the holy Mother of God whose aid was invoked through praying the Rosary—we read, (McHugh, 1982):

Prayer for the Blessed Virgin Mary

To this sort of prayer belongs the first part of the Angelic Salutation, when used by us as a prayer: *Hail Mary, full of grace, the Lord is with thee, blessed art thou among women.* For in these words we render to God the highest praise and return Him most gracious thanks, because he has bestowed all His heavenly gifts on the most Holy Virgin; and at the same time we congratulate the Virgin herself on her singular privileges.

To this form of thanksgiving the Church of God has wisely added prayers and an invocation addressed to the most holy Mother of God, by which we piously and humbly fly to her patronage, in order that, by her intercession, she may reconcile God to us sinners and may obtain for us those blessings which we stand in need of in this life and in the life to come. We, therefore, exiled children of Eve, who dwell in this vale of tears, should constantly beseech the Mother of mercy, the advocate of the faithful, to pray for us sinners. In this prayer we should earnestly implore her help and assistance; for that she possesses exalted merits with God, and that she is most desirous to assist us by her prayers, no one can doubt without impiety and wickedness. (p. 491)

Pope Leo XIII (1883) notes the efficacy of its use by St. Dominic to fight one of the great heresies.

There is none among you, venerable brethren, who will not remember how great trouble and grief God's Holy Church suffered from the Albigensian heretics, who sprung from the sect of the later Manicheans, and who filled the South of France and other portions of the Latin world with their pernicious errors, and carrying everywhere the terror of their arms, strove far and wide to rule by massacre and ruin.

Our merciful God, as you know, raised up against these most direful enemies a most holy man, the illustrious parent and founder of the Dominican Order. Great in the integrity of his doctrine, in his example of virtue, and by his apostolic labours, he proceeded undauntedly to attack the enemies of the Catholic Church, not by force of arms; but trusting wholly to that devotion which he was the first to institute under the name of the Holy Rosary, which was disseminated through the length and breadth of the earth by him and his pupils. Guided, in fact, by divine inspiration and grace, he foresaw that this devotion, like a most powerful warlike weapon, would be the means of putting the enemy to flight, and of confounding their audacity and mad impiety. Such was indeed its result. Thanks to this new method of prayer-when adopted and properly carried out as instituted by the Holy Father St. Dominic-piety, faith, and union began to return, and the projects and devices of the heretics to fall to pieces. Many wanderers also returned to the way of salvation, and the wrath of the impious was restrained by the arms of those Catholics who had determined to repel their violence. (#3)

In the same encyclical Pope Leo XIII shares the history of its papal promotion.

Thus Urban IV, testified that "every day the Rosary obtained fresh boon for Christianity." Sixtus IV declared that this method of prayer "redounded to the honour of God and the Blessed Virgin, and was well suited to obviate impending dangers;" Leo X that "it was instituted to oppose pernicious heresiarchs and heresies;" while Julius III called it "the glory of the Church." So also St. Pius V., that "with the spread of this devotion the meditations of the faithful have begun to be more inflamed, their prayers more fervent, and they have suddenly become different men; the darkness of heresy has been dissipated, and the light of Catholic faith has broken forth again." Lastly Gregory XIII in his turn pronounced that "the Rosary had been instituted by St. Dominic to appease the anger of God and to implore the intercession of the Blessed Virgin Mary." (# 5)

Pope Paul VI, (1974) notes the efficacy of the Rosary.

But there is no doubt that, after the celebration of the Liturgy of the Hours, the high point which family prayer can reach, the Rosary should be considered as one of the best and most efficacious prayers in common that the Christian family is invited to recite. (#54)

Pope John Paul II (2002) teaches us:

The Rosary mystically transports us to Mary's side as she is busy watching over the human growth of Christ in the home of Nazareth. This enables her to train us and to mold us with the same care, until Christ is "fully formed" in us (cf. *Galatians* 4:19). This role of Mary, totally grounded in that of Christ and radically subordinated to it, "in no way obscures or diminishes the unique mediation of Christ, but rather shows its power".[20] This is the luminous principle expressed by the Second Vatican Council which I have so powerfully experienced in my own life and have made the basis of my episcopal motto: *Totus Tuus*.[21] The motto is of course inspired by the teaching of Saint Louis Marie Grignion de Montfort, who explained in the following words Mary's role in the process of our configuration to Christ: *"Our entire perfection consists in being conformed, united and consecrated to Jesus Christ.* Hence the most perfect of all devotions is undoubtedly that which conforms, unites and consecrates us most perfectly to Jesus Christ. Now, since Mary is of all creatures the one most conformed to Jesus Christ, it follows that among all devotions that which most consecrates and conforms a soul to our Lord is devotion to Mary, his Holy Mother, and that the more a soul is consecrated to her the more will it be consecrated to Jesus Christ".[22] Never as in the Rosary do the life of Jesus and that of Mary appear so deeply joined. Mary lives only in Christ and for Christ! (# 15)

Thurston & Shipman (1912) describes the Rosary:

That the Rosary is pre-eminently the prayer of the people adapted alike for the use of simple and learned is proved not only by the long series of papal utterances by which it has been commended to the faithful but by the daily experience of all who are familiar with it. The objection so often made against its "vain repetitions" is felt by none but those who have failed to realize how entirely the spirit of the exercise lies in the meditation upon the fundamental mysteries of our faith. To the initiated the words of the angelical salutation form only a sort of half-conscious accompaniment, a bourdon which we may liken to the "Holy, Holy, Holy" of the heavenly choirs and surely not in itself meaningless. Neither can it be necessary to urge that the freest criticism of the historical origin of the devotion, which involves no point of doctrine, is compatible with a full appreciation of the devotional treasures which this pious exercise brings within the reach of all.

As regards the origin of the name, the word *rosarius* means a garland or bouquet of roses, and it was not infrequently used in a figurative sense — e.g. as the title of a book, to denote an anthology or collection of extracts. An early legend which after travelling all over Europe penetrated even to Abyssinia connected this name with a story of Our Lady, who was seen to take rosebuds from the lips of a young monk when he was reciting Hail Marys and to weave them into a garland which she placed upon her head. A German metrical version of this story is still extant dating from the thirteenth century. The name "Our Lady's Psalter" can also be traced back to the same period. *Corona* or *chaplet* suggests the same idea as *rosarium*. The old English name found in Chaucer and elsewhere was a "pair of beads", in which the word *bead* originally meant *prayers*. (n.p.)

On six days of my daily practice I pray the Rosary, and on Sunday I pray the Divine Mercy. On Monday through Saturday I follow the traditional schedule of the mysteries, Joyful, Sorrowful, Glorious, Luminous, Sorrowful, & Joyful. On Friday I pray the Pro-Life Rosary, and on Tuesday I pray the Rosary for the criminal.

St. Josemaria Escriva (2003) speaks of the power of the Rosary.

Today, as in other times, the Rosary must be a powerful weapon to enable us to win in our interior struggle, and to help all souls. Exalt holy Mary with your tongue: God asks you for reparation, and for praise from your lips. May you always want and know how to spread peace and happiness throughout the world, through this beautiful devotion to our Lady and through your watchful love." (p. 9)

Fr. Groeschel (2003) points us to its mystery.

We live in a time when large numbers of people have lost any sense of mystery, whereas many others harbor a simple peasant's sense of mystery even in our modern world (for example, many of the immigrants to the United States from Africa and Latin America). It is important, therefore, to reaffirm today the mysteries of Christ. Unfortunately, skepticism and rationalism in religious education have undermined the true teaching of the Catholic faith on Christ and his mysteries. Yet this is the core and foundation of our faith. In our meditations on hope, we will return to the central mystery of Christ, and we will look into what is inscrutable. We will try to plumb things that are ultimately unfathomable. And we will kneel in awe and appreciation of the little that we do know through divine revelation of the transcendent mysteries of God. (p. 20)

Five Criminal Saints

1) Saint Mary Magdalen: Feast Day, July 22
(from *Mary Magdalen in the visions of Anne Catherine Emmerich*)

Jesus, speaking in defense of Magdalen pouring the precious oil upon his head in Matthew 26: 13
"Amen, I say to you, wherever this gospel is proclaimed in the whole world, what she has done will be spoken of, in memory of her."

Mary Meditating on the Cross

1. The Family of Lazarus, Martha and Magdalen

The parents of Lazarus [the man Jesus raised from the dead, as told in the Gospel of John 11: 1-45] had in all fifteen children, of whom six died young. Of the nine that survived, only four were living at the time of Christ's teaching. These four were: Lazarus; Martha, about two years younger; Mary, looked upon as a simpleton, two years younger that Martha; and Mary Magdalen, five years younger than the simpleton. The simpleton is not named in Scripture, not reckoned among the Lazarus family; but she is known to God. She was always put aside in her family, and lived altogether unknown....

Lazarus...looked much older than Jesus; he appeared to me to be fully eight years His senior.

Lazarus had large possessions, landed property, gardens, and many servants. Martha had her own house, and another sister named Mary, who lived entirely alone, had also her separate dwelling. Magdalen lived in her castle at Magdalum. Lazarus was already long acquainted with the Holy Family. He had at an early period aided Joseph and Mary with large alms and, from first to last, did much for the Community. The purse that Judas [Iscariot] carried and all the early expenses, he supplied out of his own wealth...

2. Magdalen's Childhood

Magdalen, the youngest child, was very beautiful and, even in her early years, tall and well-developed like a girl of more advanced age. She was full of frivolity and seductive art. Her parents died when she was only seven years old. She had no great love for them even from her earliest age, on account of their severe fasts. Even as a child, she was vain beyond expression, given to petty thefts, proud, self-willed, and a lover of pleasure. She was never faithful, but clung to whatever flattered her most. She was, therefore, extravagant in her pity when her sensitive compassion was aroused, and kind and condescending to all that appealed to her senses by some external show. Her mother had had some share in Magdalen's faulty education, and that sympathetic softness the child had inherited from her.

Magdalen was spoiled by her mother and her nurse. They showed her off everywhere, caused her cleverness and pretty little ways to be admired, and sat much with her dressed up at the window. That window-sitting was the chief cause of her ruin. I saw her at the window and on the terraces of the house upon a magnificent seat of carpets and cushions, where she could be seen in all her splendor from the street. She used to steal sweetmeats, and take them to other children in the garden of the castle. Even in her ninth year she was engaged in love affairs. With her developing talents and beauty, increased also the talk and admiration they excited. She had crowds of companions. She was taught, and she wrote love verses on little rolls of parchment. I saw her while so engaged counting on her fingers. She sent these verses around, and exchanged them with her lovers. Her fame spread on all sides, and she was exceedingly admired.

But I never saw that she either really loved or was loved. It was all, on her part at least, vanity, frivolity, self-adoration, and confidence in her own beauty. I saw her a scandal to her brother and sisters whom she despised and of whom she was ashamed on account of their simple life.

3. Magdalen Inherits the Castle of Magdalum

When the patrimony was divided, the castle of Magdalum fell by lot to Magdalen. It was a very beautiful building. Magdalen had often gone there with her family when she was a very young child, and she had always entertained a special preference for it. She was only about eleven years old when, with a large household of servants, men and maids, she retired thither and set up a splendid establishment for herself.

Magdalum was a fortified place, consisting of several castles, public buildings and large squares of groves and gardens. It was eight hours east of Nazareth, about three from Capharnaum, one and a half from Bethsaida toward the south, and about a mile from the Lake of Genesareth. It was built on a slope of the mountain and extended down into the valley which stretches off toward the lake and around its shores. One of those castles belonged to Herod. He possessed a still larger one in the fertile region of Genesareth. Some of his soldiers were stationed in Magdalum, and they contributed their share to the general demoralization. The officers were on intimate terms with Magdalen. There were, besides the troops, about two hundred people in Magdalum, chiefly officials, master builders, and servants.

The castle of Magdalum was the highest and most magnificent of all; from its roof one could see across the Sea of Galilee to the opposite shore. Five roads led to Magdalum, and on every one at one half-hours distance from the well-fortified place, stood a tower built over an arch. It was like a watchtower whence could be seen far into the distance. These towers had no connection with one another; they rose out of a country covered with gardens, fields, and meadows. Magdalen had men servants and maids, fields and herds, but a very disorderly household; all went to rack and ruin.

4. Magdalen's Reputation

Sts. Zachary and Elizabeth being long since dead, St. John the Baptist has been preaching and baptizing publicly and is gaining fame and followers. Jesus has just begun His public life, but is yet to perform any miracles.

Six men who were coming from the baptism of John met Jesus. Among them were Levi, known later as Matthew, and two sons of the widowed relatives of Elizabeth. They all knew Jesus, some through relationship, others by hearsay; and they strongly suspected, though they had had no assurance of it, that He was the One of whom John had spoken. They spoke of John, of Lazarus and his sisters, especially of Magdalen. They supposed she had a devil, for she was already living apart from her family in the castle of Magdalum. These men accompanied Jesus, and were filled with astonishment at His discourse. The aspirants to baptism going from Galilee to John used to tell him all that they knew and heard of Jesus, while they that came from Ainon, where John baptized, used to tell Jesus all they knew of John...Magdalen's castle in Magdalum was not far off, and Magdalen herself was at this time at the height of her glory. (pp. 1-5)

2) Saint Dismas, Feast Day March 25 (from Wikipedia)

Saint Dismas (sometimes spelled Dysmas or only Dimas, or even Dumas), also known as the Good Thief or the Penitent Thief, is the apocryphal name given to one of the two "thieves" (Matthew 27:38) who was crucified alongside Jesus, repented of his sins, and asked Jesus to remember him in his kingdom.

The two men were crucified at the same time as Jesus, one on his right hand, and one on his left (Matthew 27:38, Mark 15:27-28, Luke 23:33, John 19:18), which Mark interprets as fulfillment of the prophecy of Isaiah 53:12. According to Matthew, both of the "thieves" at first mocked Jesus (Matthew 27:44); Luke however, mentions only that one of the "thieves" mocked him (Luke 23:39). According to the Gospel of Luke 23:39-43:

[O]ne of the malefactors which were hanged railed on him, saying, "If thou be Christ, save thyself and us." But the other answering rebuked him, saying, "Dost not thou fear God, seeing thou art in the same condemnation? And we indeed justly; for we receive the due reward of our deeds: but this man hath done nothing amiss." And he said unto Jesus, "Lord, remember me when thou comest into thy kingdom." And Jesus said unto him, "Verily I say unto thee, today shalt thou be with me in paradise." (KJV)

It should be noted that the man in question has no known name. In that the canonical Gospels were meant to be primarily a record of Jesus' life, none of the Evangelists, not even Luke who recorded the man's repentance, ever reported his name.

Regardless, later embellishments of the story elaborated on the otherwise anonymous "good thief." Dismas is his best known pseudonym and appears first in the twelfth century in the Gospel of Nicodemus. The name of "Dismas" was adapted from a Greek word meaning "sunset" or "death." The other thief's name is given as Gestas. The apocryphal Arabic Infancy Gospel calls the two thieves Titus and Dumachus, and adds a tale about how Titus (Dismas) prevented the other thieves in his company from robbing Mary and Joseph during their Flight into Egypt. In the Russian tradition the Good Thief's name is *Rakh* (Russian: Pax).

Theological significance

Though never canonized by the church, "Dismas" carries the distinction of being the only human to be canonized by Jesus himself, if by 'canonized' one means the formal recognition of a person's place in heaven. According to tradition, the Good Thief was crucified to Jesus' right hand, and the other thief was crucified to his left. For this reason, depictions of the crucifixion often show Jesus' head inclined to his right, showing his acceptance of the Good Thief. In the Russian Orthodox Church, both crucifixes and crosses are usually made with three bars: the top one, representing the titulus (the inscription that Pontius Pilate wrote and was nailed above Jesus' head; the longer crossbar on which Jesus' hands were nailed; and a slanted bar at the bottom representing the footrest to which Jesus' feet were nailed. The footrest is slanted, pointing up towards the Good Thief, and pointing down towards the other.

The biblical account of the repentant thief is foundational to the teaching of the church regarding Baptism of desire, whereby one who desires baptism, but is prevented by circumstances beyond his control from actually being baptized, may be saved by the grace and mercy of God. Traditionalist Catholics who argue that the Church has never taught Baptism of Desire say that the Dismas died and was saved under the Old Law, not under the New Law in which all must be baptized.

Legacy

Patriarch Theophilus of Alexandria (385-412) wrote a *Homily on the Crucifixion and the Good Thief*, which is a classic of Coptic literature.

In the Eastern Orthodox Church, one of the most moving hymns of Good Friday is entitled, *The Good Thief* (or *The Wise Thief*, Church Slavonic: *Razboinika blagorazumnago*), and speaks of how Christ granted Dismas Paradise. There are several moving compositions of this hymn which are used in the Russian Orthodox Church and form one of the highlights of the Matins service on Good Friday.

In medieval art, St Dismas is often depicted as accompanying Jesus in the Harrowing of Hell as related in 1 Peter 3:19–20 and the Apostles' Creed (though neither text mentions the thief).

A number of towns, including San Dimas, California, are named after him, and the Christian rock band Dizmas named themselves after the "good thief" in recognition of his decision on the Cross to follow Christ. There also exist parish churches named after him, such as the Church of the Good Thief in Kingston, Ontario, Canada.

As part of Christ's story Dismas often appears in cinematic portrayals though with varying degrees of importance. He sometimes appears as just a background character whose presence in the film is limited to his role in Luke's Gospel, if that much. One exception was Cecil B. DeMille's 1927 *The King of Kings* where his fate is compared to Jesus'. While in one scene people are mourning for Jesus as He is en route to Golgotha, in the next scene the very same people are throwing garbage as Dismas and Gestas, the "bad thief." Later when all three men are crucified, Dismas defends Jesus from Gestas' insults and asks to be forgiven for his own crimes. Jesus forgives Dismas. Later when the two men are dead, Mary is mourning at the foot of her Son's cross. She notices that at the foot of Dismas' cross is a disheveled old woman crying for Dismas. The old woman says "He was my son." The two mothers embrace and console each other.

In 1961's *King of Kings*, Dismas and Gestas, along with Barrabas, are awaiting their fates. Dismas and Gestas are appalled when Barrabbas compares himself to them. They say "We're only thieves! You're a murderer!" (He and Gestas say this regardless of the fact that there is every chance that the real "Dismas" was just as violent as Barrabas and no mere thief. This is ironic considering that this *King of Kings* emphasized the political climate of first century Israel.)

A major part of Dismas' legacy is one of penance. Though a rebel and perhaps even a terrorist and not a thief, the fact that he did live a wicked life and was sorry for that life means that the traditional moral drawn from his story is still intact. Symbolic of this it is very common for prison chapels to be dedicated to Saint Dismas, since he represents not only the epitome of a repentant malefactor, but also God's willingness to forgive even at the last moment. This is meant to convey that with the love of God, it is never too late. (Retrieved March 30 from http://en.wikipedia.org/wiki/Saint_Dismas)

3) Saint Callistus, Feast Day October 14
(from New Advent)

Pope Callistus I

(Written by most Latins, Augustine, Optatus, etc. CALLIXTUS or CALIXTUS).

Martyr, died c. 223. His contemporary, Julius Africanus, gives the date of his accession as the first (or second?) year of Elagabalus, i.e., 218 or 219. Eusebius and the Liberian catalogue agree in giving him five years of episcopate. His Acts are spurious, but he is the earliest pope found the fourth-century "Depositio Martirum", and this is good evidence that he was really a martyr, although he lived in a time of peace under Alexander Severus, whose mother was a Christian. We learn from the "Historiae Augustae" that a spot on which he had built an oratory was claimed by the tavern-keepers, *popinarii*, but the emperor decided that the worship of any god was better than a tavern. This is said to have been the origin of Sta. Maria in Trastevere, which was built, according to the Liberian catalogue, by Pope Julius. In fact the Church of St. Callistus is close by, containing a well into which legend says his body was thrown, and this is probably the church he built, rather than the more famous basilica. He was buried in the cemetery of Calepodius on the Aurelian Way, and his anniversary is given by the "Depositio Martirum" (*Callisti in viâ Aureliâ miliario III*) and by the subsequent martyrologies on 14 October, on which day his feast is still kept. His relics were translated in the ninth century to Sta. Maria in Trastevere.

Our chief knowledge of this pope is from his bitter enemies, Tertullian and the antipope who wrote the "Philosophumena", no doubt Hippolytus. Their calumnies are probably based on facts. According to the "Philosophumena" (c. ix) Callistus was the slave of Carpophorus, a Christian of the household of Caesar. His master entrusted large sums of money to Callistus, with which he started a bank in which brethren and widows lodged money, all of which Callistus lost. He took to flight. Carpophorus followed him to Portus, where Callistus had embarked on a ship. Seeing his master approach in a boat, the slave jumped into the sea, but was prevented from drowning himself, dragged ashore, and consigned to the punishment reserved for slaves, the *pistrinum*, or hand-mill. The brethren, believing that he still had money in his name, begged that he might be released. But he had nothing, so he again courted death by insulting the Jews at their synagogue. The Jews haled him before the prefect Fuscianus. Carpophorus declared that Callistus was not to be looked upon as a Christian, but he was thought to be trying to save his slave, and Callistus was sent to the mines in Sardinia. Some time after this, Marcia, the mistress of Commodus, sent for Pope Victor and asked if there were any martyrs in Sardinia. He gave her the list, without including Callistus. Marcia sent a eunuch who was a priest (or "old man") to release the prisoners. Callistus fell at his feet, and persuaded him to take him also. Victor was annoyed; but being a compassionate man, he kept silence. However, he sent Callistus to Antium with a monthly allowance. When Zephyrinus became pope, Callistus was recalled and set over the cemetery belonging to the Church, not a private catacomb; it has ever since borne Callistus's name. He obtained great influence over the ignorant, illiterate, and grasping Zephyrinus by bribes. We are not told how it came about that the runaway slave (now free by Roman law from his master, who had lost his rights when Callistus was condemned to penal servitude to the State) became archdeacon and then pope.

Döllinger and De Rossi have demolished this contemporary scandal. To begin with, Hippolytus does not say that Callistus by his own fault lost the money deposited with him. He evidently jumped from the vessel rather to escape than to commit suicide. That Carpophorus, a Christian, should commit a Christian slave to the horrible punishment of the *pistrinum* does not speak well for the master's character. The intercession of the Christians for Callistus is in his favour. It is absurd to suppose that he courted death by attacking a synagogue; it is clear that he asked the Jewish money-lenders to repay what they owed him, and at some risk to himself. The declaration of Carpophorus that Callistus was no Christian was scandalous and untrue. Hippolytus himself shows that it was as a Christian that Callistus was sent to the mines, and therefore as a confessor, and that it was as a Christian that he was released. If Pope Victor granted Callistus a monthly pension, he need not suppose that he regretted his release. It is unlikely that Zephyrinus was ignorant and base. Callistus could hardly have raised himself so high without considerable talents, and the vindictive spirit exhibited by Hippolytus and his defective theology explain why Zephyrinus placed his confidence rather in Callistus than in the learned disciple of Irenaeus.

The orthodoxy of Callistus is challenged by both Hippolytus and Tertullian on the ground that in a famous edict he granted Communion after due penance to those who had committed adultery and fornication. It is clear that Callistus based his decree on the power of binding and loosing granted to Peter, to his successors, and to all in communion with them: "As to thy decision", cries the Montanist Tertullian, "I ask, whence dost thou usurp this right of the Church? If it is because the Lord said to Peter: Upon this rock I will build My Church, I will give thee the keys of the kingdom of heaven', or whatsoever though bindest or loosest on earth shall be bound or loosed in heaven', that thou presumest that this power of binding and loosing has been handed down to thee also, that is to every Church in communion with Peter's (*ad omnem ecclesiam Petri propinquam*, i.e. *Petri ecclesiae propinquam*), who art thou that destroyest and alterest the manifest intention of the Lord, who conferred this on Peter personally and alone?" (De Pudicitia, xxi.) The edict was an order to the whole Church (ib., i): "I hear that an edict has been published, and a peremptory one; the bishop of bishops, which means the Pontifex Maximus, proclaims: I remit the crimes of adultery and fornication to those who have done penance." Doubtless Hippolytus and Tertullian were upholding a supposed custom of earlier times, and the pope in decreeing a relaxation was regarded as enacting a new law. On this point it is unnecessary to justify Callistus. Other complaints of Hippolytus are that Callistus did not put converts from heresy to public penance for sins committed outside the

Church (this mildness was customary in St. Augustine's time); that he had received into his "school" (i.e. The Catholic Church) those whom Hippolytus had excommunicated from "The Church" (i.e., his own sect); that he declared that a mortal sin was not ("always", we may supply) a sufficient reason for deposing a bishop. Tertullian (De Exhort. Castitatis, vii) speaks with reprobation of bishops who had been married more than once, and Hippolytus charges Callistus with being the first to allow this, against St. Paul's rule. But in the East marriages before baptism were not counted, and in any case the law is one from which the pope can dispense if necessity arise. Again Callistus allowed the lower clergy to marry, and permitted noble ladies to marry low persons and slaves, which by the Roman law was forbidden; he had thus given occasion for infanticide. Here again Callistus was rightly insisting on the distinction between the ecclesiastical law of marriage and the civil law, which later ages have always taught.. Hippolytus also declared that rebaptizing (of heretics) was performed first in Callistus's day, but he does not state that Callistus was answerable for this. On the whole, then, it is clear that the Catholic Church sides with Callistus against the schismatic Hippolytus and the heretic Tertullian. Not a word is said against the character of Callistus since his promotion, nor against the validity of his election.

Hippolytus, however, regards Callistus as a heretic. Now Hippolytus's own Christology is most imperfect, and he tells us that Callistus accused him of Ditheism. It is not to be wondered at, then, if he calls Callistus the inventor of a kind of modified Sabellianism. In reality it is certain that Zephyrinus and Callistus condemned various Monarchians and Sabellius himself, as well as the opposite error of Hippolytus. This is enough to suggest that Callistus held the Catholic Faith. And in fact it cannot be denied that the Church of Rome must have held a Trinitarian doctrine not far from that taught by Callistus's elder contemporary Tertullian and by his much younger contemporary Novatian—a doctrine which was not so explicitly taught in the greater part of the East for a long period afterwards. The accusations of Hippolytus speak for the sure tradition of the Roman Church and for its perfect orthodoxy and moderation. If we knew more of St. Callistus from Catholic sources, he would probably appear as one of the greatest of the popes. (Retrieved March 30, 2010 from http://www.newadvent.org/cathen/03183d.htm)

4) St. Mary of Egypt, Feast Day April 3
(from Wikipedia)

Mary of Egypt (ca. 344 – ca. 421) is revered as the patron saint of penitents, most particularly in the Eastern Orthodox, Oriental Orthodox, and Eastern Catholic churches, as well as in the Roman Catholic and Anglican churches.

The primary source of information on Saint Mary of Egypt is the *Vita* written of her by St. Sophronius, the Patriarch of Jerusalem (634 - 638). Most of the information in this section is taken from this source.

127

Saint Mary, also know as Maria Aegyptica, was born somewhere in Egypt, and at the age of twelve ran away to the city of Alexandria where she lived an extremely dissolute life. Some authorities refer to her as a prostitute during this period, but in her *Vita* she states that she often refused the money offered for her sexual favors. She was, she said, driven "by an insatiable desire and an irrepressible passion," and that she mainly lived by begging, supplemented by spinning flax.

After seventeen years of this lifestyle, she travelled to Jerusalem for the Feast of the Exaltation of the Holy Cross. She undertook the journey as a sort of "anti-pilgrimage," stating that she hoped to find in the pilgrim crowds at Jerusalem even more partners in her lust. She paid for her passage by offering sexual favors to other pilgrims, and she continued her habitual lifestyle for a short time in Jerusalem. Her *Vita* relates that when she tried to enter the Church of the Holy Sepulcher for the celebration, she was barred from doing so by an unseen force. Realizing that this was because of her impurity, she was struck with remorse, and on seeing an icon of the Theotokos (the Virgin Mary) outside the church, she prayed for forgiveness and promised to give up the world (i.e., become an ascetic). Then she attempted again to enter the church, and this time was permitted in. After venerating the relic of the true cross, she returned to the icon to give thanks, and heard a voice telling her, "If you cross the Jordan, you will find glorious rest/ true peace." She immediately went to the monastery of St. John the Baptist on the bank of the River Jordan, where she received absolution and afterwards Holy Communion. The next morning, she crossed the Jordan and retired to the desert to live the rest of her life as a hermit in penitence. She took with her only three loaves of bread, and once they were gone, lived only on what she could find in the wilderness.

Approximately one year before her death, she recounted her life to St. Zosimas of Palestine who encountered her in the desert. When he unexpectedly met her in the desert, she was completely naked and almost unrecognizable as human. She asked Zosimas to toss her his mantle to cover herself with, and then she narrated her life's story to him, manifesting marvellous clairvoyance. She asked him to meet her at the banks of the Jordan on Holy Thursday of the following year, and bring her Holy Communion. When he fulfilled her wish, she crossed the river to get to him by walking on the surface of the water and received Holy Communion, telling him to meet her again in the desert the following Lent. The next year, Zosimas travelled to the same spot where he first met her, some twenty day's journey from his monastery, and found her lying there dead. According to an inscription written in the sand next to her head, she had died on the very night he had given her Communion and had been somehow miraculously transported to the place he found her, and her body preserved incorrupt. He buried her body with the assistance of a passing lion. On returning to the monastery he related her life story to the brethren, and it was preserved among them as oral tradition until it was written down by St. Sophronius.

Date of death

There is disagreement among various sources regarding the dates of St. Mary's life. The dates given above correspond to those in the Catholic Encyclopedia. The Bollandists place her death in 421, others give the date of her death as 522 (see Orthodox Wiki article, below), or 530 (see *Prolog from Ohrid*, April 1). The only clue given in her *Vita* is the fact that the day of her repose was April 1, which is stated to be Holy Thursday, meaning that Easter fell on April 4 that year.

If one consults a perpetual calendar that is keyed to the Julian Calendar (the one in use at the time), one finds that there are 24 years in the relevant centuries on which April 1 occurs on a Thursday. Of these, the years on which Easter would fall on April 4 according to the Julian Calendar are: 443, 454, 527, 538, and 549.

It is notable that the Synaxarion states that Zosimas lived during the reign of the Emperor Theodosius the Younger, who reigned from 408 to 450. According to tradition, Zosimas lived almost a hundred years, dying in the sixth century, and the *Vita* states that he was fifty-three years old when he met St. Mary.

Religious commemoration

The Temple of Portunus in Rome was preserved by being rededicated to Saint Mary of Egypt in 872.

In iconography St. Mary of Egypt is depicted as a deeply tanned, emaciated old woman with unkempt gray hair, either naked or covered by the mantle she borrowed from Zosimas. She is often shown with the three loaves of bread she bought before undertaking her journey into the desert.

Her feast day is kept by the Orthodox according to the Fixed Cycle on April 1. On the Moveable Cycle the Orthodox Church also commemorates her on the fifth Sunday of Great Lent, on which day it is customary for the priest to bless dried fruit after the Divine Liturgy. The *Life of St. Mary* by St. Sophronius is appointed to be read during the Matins of the Great Canon of St. Andrew of Crete on the preceding Thursday.

In the Roman Catholic Church, she is commemorated on April 3 (or April 2, according to the Roman Martyrology). Although she is venerated by Anglicans, St. Mary of Egypt does not appear on Anglican Church Calendars.

There is a chapel dedicated to her at the Church of the Holy Sepulcher in Jerusalem, commemorating the moment of her conversion. (Retrieved April 2,

2010 from
http://en.wikipedia.org/wiki/Mary_of_Egypt)

5) 𝕾aint Paul Hanh, Feast Day May 28
(from *Magnificat*)

Martyr (1826-1849)
A Vietnamese martyr. A convert to Catholicism, Paul later fell away from the faith and became a member of an outlaw band. Captured by the government, he proclaimed his faith and was thus singled out for especially cruel treatment. After enduring tortures, he was beheaded near Saigon.
(Retrieved April 2, 2010 from
http://www.catholic.org/saints/saint.php?saint_id=5265)

Paul Hanh, of Cho Quan, Vietnam, fell away from the practice of his Catholic faith, joining a gang of outlaws. But amidst his criminal activities as a bandit, he secretly lent assistance to his fellow Catholics suffering cruel persecution under the Emperor Tu Duc. Eventually Paul was arrested for his thievery. Repenting of his crimes, he openly professed his Catholic identity before the pagan authorities. Brutal tortures failed to make him deny the faith he had formerly neglected to live by. On May 28, 1859, Paul was beheaded for being a Christian."

Magnificat, May 2009, Volume 11, No. 3, (p. 384)

Praying the Rosary for the Criminal

Prayer to St. Michael for Protection of The Catholic Church and Her Members

✠ **Glorious St. Michael**, Guardian and Defender of the Catholic Church, come to her assistance, against which the powers of Hell are unchained. Guard with thy special care her august visible head, Our Holy Father, and obtain for him and for us that the hour of triumph may speedily arrive.

O Glorious Archangel St. Michael, watch over us during life, defend us against the assaults of the demon, assist us especially at the hour of death, obtain for us a favorable judgment and the happiness of beholding God face to face for endless ages. Amen.

I unite myself with all the saints in Heaven, and with all the just on earth; I unite myself with Thee, my Jesus, in order to praise Thy Holy Mother worthily and to praise Thee in Her and by Her. I renounce all the distractions that may come to me while I am saying the Rosary today, for the criminal.

Prayer for Priests and Nuns

O Jesus, our great High Priest, hear my humble prayer on behalf of your servants. Give all priests and all nuns a deep faith, a bright and firm hope, and a burning love which will ever increase in the course of their life. In their loneliness, comfort them. In their sorrows, strengthen them. In their frustrations, point out to them that it is through suffering that the soul is purified, and show them that they are needed by the Church; they are needed by souls; they are needed for the work of redemption.

O Loving Mother Mary, Mother of priests and nuns, take to your heart your children who are close to you because of the power which they have received to carry on the work of Christ in a world which needs them so much. Be their comfort, be their joy, be their strength, and especially help them to live and to defend the ideals of consecrated celibacy. Amen

In the name of the Father, and of the Son, and of the Holy Spirit. Amen

St. Callistus, penitential criminal, who became Peter, bless all penitential criminals that we live in the light of God, as did you during your pontifical welcome to the redeemed sinner, and bring us peace and guidance in our search for God. Amen

O Blessed Virgin Mary, we offer Thee this Creed in order to honor the faith that Thou didst have upon earth and to ask Thee to have us share in the same faith.

I believe in God, the Father Almighty, Creator of heaven and earth; and in Jesus Christ, His only

Son, our Lord; Who was conceived by the Holy Spirit, born of the Virgin Mary, suffered under Pontius Pilate, was crucified, died, and was buried. He descended into hell; the third day He arose again from the dead. He ascended into heaven, and sits at the right hand of God, the Father Almighty; from thence He shall come to judge the living and the dead. I believe in the Holy Spirit, the Holy Catholic Church, the communion of Saints, the forgiveness of sins, the resurrection of the body and life everlasting. Amen.

Saint Dismas, penitential criminal, first canonized saint of the Church, your grace came from your suffering with Christ on Golgotha where he forgave you and took you with him to heaven, *this day.* Please intercede for all criminals to obtain grace to repent of our sins and be with Christ in heaven. Amen

O Lord, we offer Thee this Our Father so as to adore Thee in Thy Oneness and to recognize Thee as the First Cause and the Last End of all things.

Our Father, who art in heaven; hallowed be Thy name; Thy kingdom come; Thy will be done on earth as it is in heaven. Give us this day our daily bread; and forgive us our trespasses as we forgive those who trespass against us, and lead us not into temptation; but deliver us from evil. Amen.

Most Holy Trinity, we offer Thee these three Hail Marys so as to thank Thee for all the graces which Thou hast given to Mary and those which Thou hast given us through Her intercession.

Hail Mary, full of grace, the Lord is with thee; blessed art thou among women, and blessed is the fruit of thy womb, Jesus. Holy Mary, Mother of God, pray for us sinners, now and at the hour of our death. Amen.

Saint Mary Magdalene, penitential criminal, apostle to the apostles, who Christ proclaimed as the model of penance, and who by your faith and devotion became the first, after our Holy Mother, to see our Lord after his resurrection, sharing in Christ's glorious presence. Please intercede for all criminals that we may someday share everlasting joy through our penance and redemption. Amen.

Glory be to the Father, and to the Son, and to the Holy Spirit. As it was in the beginning, is now, and ever shall be, world without end. Amen.

First Sorrowful Mystery
The Agony in the Garden
St. Luke

22: 39 Then going out he went, as was his custom, to the Mount of Olives, and the disciples followed him. **40** When he arrived at the place he said to them, "Pray that you may not undergo the test." **41** After withdrawing about a stone's throw from them and kneeling, he prayed, **42** saying, "Father, if you are willing, take this cup away from me; still, not my will but yours be done." **43** And to strengthen him an angel from heaven appeared to him. **44** He was in such agony and he prayed so fervently that his sweat became like drops of blood falling on the ground. **45** When he rose from prayer and returned to his disciples, he found them sleeping from grief. **46** He said to them, "Why are you sleeping? Get up and pray that you may not undergo the test."

Our Father, who art in heaven; hallowed be Thy name; Thy kingdom come; Thy will be done on earth as it is in heaven. Give us this day our daily bread; and forgive us our trespasses as we forgive those who trespass against us, and lead us not into temptation; but deliver us from evil. Amen

Hail Mary, full of grace, the Lord is with thee; blessed art thou among women, and blessed is the fruit of thy womb, Jesus. Holy Mary, Mother of God, pray for us sinners, now and at the hour of our death. Amen.

O my Jesus, forgive us our sins, save us from the fires of hell. Lead all souls to heaven, especially those most in need of your mercy. **Glory be** to the Father, and to the Son, and to the Holy Spirit. As it was in the beginning, is now, and ever shall be, world without end. Amen.

Second Sorrowful Mystery
The Scourging at the Pillar
St. Mark

15: 12 Pilate again said to them in reply, "Then what do you want me to do with the man you call the king of the Jews?" **13** They shouted again, "Crucify him." **14** Pilate said to them, "Why? What evil has he done?" They only shouted the louder, "Crucify him." **15** So Pilate, wishing to satisfy the crowd, released Barabbas to them and, after he had Jesus scourged, handed him over to be crucified.

Our Father, who art in heaven; hallowed be Thy name; Thy kingdom come; Thy will be done on earth as it is in heaven. Give us this day our daily bread; and forgive us our trespasses as we forgive those who trespass against us, and lead us not into temptation; but deliver us from evil. Amen

Hail Mary, full of grace, the Lord is with thee; blessed art thou among women, and blessed is the fruit of thy womb, Jesus. Holy Mary, Mother of God, pray for us sinners, now and at the hour of our death. Amen.

O my Jesus, forgive us our sins, save us from the fires of hell. Lead all souls to heaven, especially those most in need of your mercy. **Glory be** to the Father, and to the Son, and to the Holy Spirit. As it was in the beginning, is now, and ever shall be, world without end. Amen.

Third Sorrowful Mystery
The Crowning With Thorns
St. Mark

15:16 The soldiers led him away inside the palace, that is, the praetorium, and assembled the whole cohort. **17** They clothed him in purple and, weaving a crown of thorns, placed it on him. **18** They began to salute him with, "Hail, King of the Jews!" **19** and kept striking his head with a reed and spitting upon him. They knelt before him in homage.

Our Father, who art in heaven; hallowed be Thy name; Thy kingdom come; Thy will be done on earth as it is in heaven. Give us this day our daily bread; and forgive us our trespasses as we forgive those who trespass against us, and lead us not into temptation; but deliver us from evil. Amen

Hail Mary, full of grace, the Lord is with thee; blessed art thou among women, and blessed is the fruit of thy womb, Jesus. Holy Mary, Mother of God, pray for us sinners, now and at the hour of our death. Amen.

O my Jesus, forgive us our sins, save us from the fires of hell. Lead all souls to heaven, especially those most in need of your mercy. **Glory be** to the Father, and to the Son, and to the Holy Spirit. As it was in the beginning, is now, and ever shall be, world without end. Amen.

Fourth Sorrowful Mystery
The Carrying of the Cross
St. Mark

15: 20 And when they had mocked him, they stripped him of the purple cloak, dressed him in his own clothes, and led him out to crucify him. **21** They pressed into service a passer-by, Simon, a Cyrenian, who was coming in from the country, the father of Alexander and Rufus, to carry his cross. **22** They brought him to the place of Golgotha which is translated Place of the Skull.

Our Father, who art in heaven; hallowed be Thy name; Thy kingdom come; Thy will be done on earth as it is in heaven. Give us this day our daily bread; and forgive us our trespasses as we forgive those who trespass against us, and lead us not into temptation; but deliver us from evil. Amen

Hail Mary, full of grace, the Lord is with thee; blessed art thou among women, and blessed is the fruit of thy womb, Jesus. Holy Mary, Mother of God, pray for us sinners, now and at the hour of our death. Amen.

O my Jesus, forgive us our sins, save us from the fires of hell. Lead all souls to heaven, especially those most in need of your mercy. **Glory be** to the Father, and to the Son, and to the Holy Spirit. As it was in the beginning, is now, and ever shall be, world without end. Amen.

Fifth Sorrowful Mystery
The Crucifixion
St. Luke & St. John

32 Now two others, both criminals, were led away with him to be executed. **33** When they came to the place called the Skull, they crucified him and the criminals there, one on his right, the other on his left. **34** Then Jesus said, "Father, forgive them, they know not what they do." They divided his garments by casting lots. **35** The people stood by and watched; the rulers, meanwhile, sneered at him and said, "He saved others, let him save himself if he is the chosen one, the Messiah of God." **36** Even the soldiers jeered at him. As they approached to offer him wine **37** they called out, "If you are King of the Jews, save yourself." **38** Above him there was an inscription that read, "This is the King of the Jews." **39** Now one of the criminals hanging there reviled Jesus, saying, "Are you not the Messiah? Save yourself and us." **40** The other, however, rebuking him, said in reply, "Have you no fear of God, for you are subject to the same condemnation? **41** And indeed, we have been condemned justly, for the sentence we received corresponds to our crimes, but this man has done nothing criminal." **42** Then he said, "Jesus, remember me when you come into your kingdom." **43** He replied to him, "Amen, I say to you, today you will be with me in Paradise." **44** It was now about noon and darkness came over the whole land until three in the afternoon **45** because of an eclipse of the sun. Then the veil of the temple was torn down the middle. **46** Jesus cried out in a loud voice, "Father, into your hands I commend my spirit"; and when he had said this he breathed his last. **John 19:25** Standing by the cross of Jesus were his mother and his mother's sister, Mary the wife of Clopas, and Mary of Magdala.

Our Father, who art in heaven; hallowed be Thy name; Thy kingdom come; Thy will be done on earth as it is in heaven. Give us this day our daily bread; and forgive us our trespasses as we forgive those who trespass against us, and lead us not into temptation; but deliver us from evil. Amen

Hail Mary, full of grace, the Lord is with thee; blessed art thou among women, and blessed is the fruit of thy womb, Jesus. Holy Mary, Mother of God, pray for us sinners, now and at the hour of our death. Amen.

O my Jesus, forgive us our sins, save us from the fires of hell. Lead all souls to heaven, especially those most in need of your mercy. **Glory be** to the Father, and to the Son, and to the Holy Spirit. As it was in the beginning, is now, and ever shall be, world without end. Amen.

O God, whose only begotten Son, by his life, death and resurrection, has purchased for us the rewards of eternal life, grant, we beseech you, that through meditating on these mysteries in the most Holy Rosary of the Blessed Virgin Mary, we may imitate what they contain, and obtain what they promise. Through Christ our Lord. Amen.

Saint Paul Hanh, penitential criminal, your service, while still a criminal, to Catholics being persecuted in Vietnam, and after your conversion to Catholicism, your martyrdom, is a heavenly model, and I implore you to help penitential criminals struggling for grace and redemption. Amen

Saint Mary of Egypt, penitential criminal, the True Cross called out to you at the door of the Church, you walked across the waters of the River Jordan to receive the eucharist from Abbot Zosimus after 47 years of contemplation and prayer in the desert, intercede for penitential criminals that we may follow you in the path to redemption. Amen

Glorious Saint Dismas, you alone of all the great Penitent Saints were directly canonized by Christ Himself; you were assured of a place in Heaven with Him "*this day*" because of the sincere confession of your sins to Him in the tribunal of Calvary and your true sorrow for them as you hung beside Him in that open confessional; you who by your direct love and repentance did open the Heart of Jesus in mercy and forgiveness even before the centurion's spear tore it asunder; you whose face was closer to that of Jesus in His last agony, to offer Him a word of comfort, closer even than that of His Beloved Mother, Mary; you who knew so well how to pray, teach me the words to say to Him to gain pardon and the grace of perseverance; and you who are so close to Him now in Heaven, as you were during His last moments on earth, pray to Him for me that I shall never again desert Him, but that at the close of my life I may hear from Him the words He addressed to you: "This day thou shalt be with Me in Paradise." Amen.

Most Sacred Heart of Jesus, truly present in the Holy Eucharist, I consecrate my body and soul to be entirely one with Your Heart being sacrificed at every instant on all the altars of the world and giving praise to the Father, pleading for the coming of His Kingdom. Please receive this humble offering of myself. Use me as You will for the glory of the Father and the salvation of souls. Most holy Mother of God, never let me be separated from your Divine Son. Please protect me, my family, and all the faithful as your special children. Amen.

_____

_____

_____

References-Abbreviations

CA   *Centesimus Annus*, Pope John Paul II, Encyclical (1991)

CCC1   Catechism of the Catholic Church, Pope John Paul II, Vatican II, (First Edition 1992)

CCC2   *Catechism of the Catholic Church*, Pope John Paul II, Vatican II, (Second Edition 1997)

CCT   *Catechism of the Council of Trent* Pope Pius V, (1566)

CL   *Christifideles Laici* Pope John Paul II, Apostolic Exhortation (1988)

CSDC   *Compendium of the Social Doctrine of the Church*, Pontifical Council *Justitia et Pax*, (2004)

CSWT   *Christian Social Witness and Teaching: The Catholic Tradition from Genesis to Centesimus Annus* by Rodger Charles S.J. (1998)

CIV   *Caritas in Veritate,* Pope Benedict XVI, Encyclical, (2009)

DCE   *Deus Caritas Est,* Pope Benedict XVI, Encyclical (2005)

LE   *Laborem Exercens*, Pope John Paul II, Encyclical, (1981)

GES   *Gaudium et Spes,* Pope Paul VI, Pastoral Constitution, (1965)

MEM   *Mater et Magistra,* Pope John XXIII, Encyclical, (1961)

OA   *Octogesima Adveniens,* Pope Paul VI, Apostolic Letter, (1971)

PP	*Populorum Progressio*, Pope Paul VI, Encyclical, (1967)
QA	*Quadragesimo Anno,* Pope Pius XI, Encyclical, (1931)
QAM	*Quod Apostolici Muneris,* Pope Leo XII, Encyclical (1878)
RN	*Rerum Novarum,* Pope Leo XIII, Encyclical, (1891)
SC	*Sacrosanctum Concilium*, Pope Paul VI. Constitution on the Sacred Liturgy, Vatican II, (1963).
SD	*Salvifici Doloris,* Pope John Paul II, Apostolic Letter. (1984)
SE	*Spiritual Exercises of St. Ignatius,* Translated by Louis J. Puhl, S. J. (1951)
SRS	*Sollicitudo Rei Socialis*, Pope John Paul II, Encyclical (1987)
SS	*Spe Salvi,* Pope Benedict XVI, Encyclical, (2007)
ST	*Summa Theologica,* St. Thomas Aquinas, (1274)

References-Bibliography

Adam, K. (1935). *The spirit of Catholicism*. New
    York: The Macmillan Company.

Barthel, M. (1984). *The Jesuits: History and
    legend of the Society of Jesus*. New York:
    William Morrow & Company.

Bornstein, D. (2004). *How to change the world:
    Social entrepreneurs and the power of new
    ideas*. New York: Oxford University Press.

Bowman, J. (2006). *Honor: A history*. New York;
    Encounter Books.

Burnett, P. H. (2004). [1860]. *The true church: The
    path which led a Protestant lawyer to the
    Catholic Church*. Antioch, California: Solas
    Press.

Chautard, D. J-B. (1946). *The soul of the
    apostolate*. Trappist, Kentucky: Abbey of
    Gethsemani.

Delp, A. (2006). *Alfred Delp, SJ. priest and
    martyr: Advent of the heart, Seasonal
    sermons and prison writings 1941-1944*. (A.
    S. Walburg, Trans.). San Francisco: Ignatius
    Press.

Emmerich, A. C. (2005). [1914] *Mary Magdalen in
    the visions of Anne Catherine Emmerich*,
    Rockford, Illinois: Tan Books And
    Publishers, Inc.

Escriva, J. (2003). *Holy rosary*. London: Scepter.

Groeschel, B. J. (2003). *The Rosary: Chain of
    hope*. San Francisco: Ignatius Press.

Guardini, R. (1956). *The Lord*. London: Longmans.

Jaki, S. L. (1997). *And on this rock: The witness of*

147

one land and two covenants. Front Royal, Virginia: Christendom Press.

McHugh. J.A. & Callan, C. J., Trans.). (1982). *Catechism of the Council of Trent*, Rockford, Illinois: Tan Books and Publishers.

Murray J. C. (1960). *We hold these truths: Catholic reflections on the American proposition.* New York: Sheed and Ward

Pope Benedict XVI. (2007). *Jesus of Nazareth: From the baptism in the Jordan to the Transfiguration.* New York: Doubleday.

Pope John Paul II. (2002) Apostolic Letter, *Rosarium Virginis Mariea*, Retrieved April 2, 2010 from http://www.vatican.va/holy_father/john_paul_ii/apost_letters/documents/hf_jp-ii_apl_20021016_rosarium-virginis-mariae_en.html

Pope Leo XIII. (1883) Encyclical, *Supremi Apostolatus Officio* Retrieved April 2, 2010 from http://www.vatican.va/holy_father/leo_xiii/encyclicals/documents/hf_l-xiii_enc_01091883_supremi-apostolatus-officio_en.html

Pope Paul VI. (1974). Apostolic Exhortation, *Marialus Cultus,* Retrieved April 2, 2010 from http://www.vatican.va/holy_father/paul_vi/apost_exhortations/documents/hf_p-vi_exh_19740202_marialis-cultus_en.html

Saint-Exupery, A.D. (1950). *The wisdom of the sands.* (S. Gilbert, Trans.). New York: Harcourt Brace.

Skotnicki, A. (2008). *Criminal justice and the Catholic Church*. (New York: Rowman & Littlefield Publishers.

Thurston, H., & Shipman, A. (1912). The Rosary. In *The Catholic Encyclopedia*. New York: Robert Appleton Company. Retrieved March 31, 2010 from New Advent: http://www.newadvent.org/cathen/13184b.htm

Tsunetomo, Y. (2002). *Hagakure: The book of the Samurai*. (Translated by Scott Wilson). Kodansha International: Tokyo.

Tugwell, S. (March 2010). Day by day: What drove the woman, *Magnificat, 11*(14), 316-317.

Tyerman, C. (2006). *God's War*: A new history of the crusades. Cambridge, Massachusetts: Harvard University Press.

Zehr, H. (2002). *The little book of restorative justice*. Intercourse, Pennsylvania: Good Books.

About the Author

David H. Lukenbill was a criminal—thief and robber—for 20 years, serving 12 of those years in maximum security federal and state prisons. He eventually transformed himself through education, (AA in Criminal Justice—Sacramento City College; BS in Organizational Behavior and Masters in Public Administration—University of San Francisco) many years developing and working with criminal transformative organizations (including founding and directing, for three years, one of the most successful college-based programs for former criminals in California) studying the social teaching, and God's grace discovering and being baptized into the Catholic Church.

He is married to his wife of 27 years and they have one child. They live by the American River in California with two cats, and all the wild critters they can feed.

Contact information at the Lampstand Foundation website, www.lampstandfoundation.org

Prayer to St. Dismas

Glorious Saint Dismas, you alone of all the great Penitent Saints were directly canonized by Christ Himself; you were assured of a place in Heaven with Him "*this day*" because of the sincere confession of your sins to Him in the tribunal of Calvary and your true sorrow for them as you hung beside Him in that open confessional; you who by the direct sword thrust of your love and repentance did open the Heart of Jesus in mercy and forgiveness even before the centurion's spear tore it asunder; you whose face was closer to that of Jesus in His last agony, to offer Him a word of comfort, closer even than that of His Beloved Mother, Mary; you who knew so well how to pray, teach me the words to say to Him to gain pardon and the grace of perseverance; and you who are so close to Him now in Heaven, as you were during His last moments on earth, pray to Him for me that I shall never again desert Him, but that at the close of my life I may hear from Him the words He addressed to you: "This day thou shalt be with Me in Paradise." Amen.

Prayer to St. Michael

✠ Glorious St. Michael, Guardian and Defender of the Church of Jesus Christ, come to the assistance of the Church, against which the powers of Hell are unchained. Guard with thy special care her august visible head, and obtain for him and for us that the hour of triumph may speedily arrive.

✠ Glorious Archangel St. Michael, watch over us during life, defend us against the assaults of the demon, assist us especially at the hour of death, obtain for us a favorable judgment and the happiness of beholding God face to face for endless ages. Amen.